COMMON EXPERIENCE
AND THE
ACCOMMODATION
OF
DIFFERENCES

To Deanna, Justin, Louise and Ethan.

TABLE OF CONTENTS

CHAPTER 1
AN INTRODUCTION

The Anglican Church seems to take perverse delight in teetering on the brink of schism. From the days of Henry the VIII, one controversy after another has forced the church to tread carefully along the edge of theological and ecclesiastical division. Issues concerning the divine right of kings, the nature of the Eucharist, the threefold office of ordination, and so forth have caused the church to find ways of striving to resolve seemingly irreconcilable differences that are both accommodating to the conflicting sides while being faithful to the Gospel of Christ. Currently there are many conflicts in the Anglican Communion (the ordination of women and lay presidency of the Eucharist are two examples). However, the most controversial issues concern human sexuality, specifically the blessing of same sex relationships, and the ordination of non-celibate gays and lesbians. The new Archbishop of Canterbury, Rowan Williams, has the task of keeping the Anglican Communion united in the midst of the current threat of schism. This chore is difficult because he has little actual power, other than the prestige of his office, and the opposing forces, particularly on the subject of sexuality, are firmly entrenched in their positions.

Initially it must be noted that Rowan Williams is an outsider. It is difficult for other outsiders to understand the significance of a Welshman heading the Church of England, but his appointment speaks of significant change in the office. As Archbishop of Canterbury, he is head of the southern geographic region of England, a position which carries a good deal of official authority, and the larger international Anglican Communion over which he has limited authority. As Stephen Bates of *The Guardian* observed, the Anglican Communion is "fissiparous."[1] Bates notes that the diminishing number of faithful members in the northern hemisphere is causing the churches of England and America, in particular, to lose influence while the explosion

---

[1] Stephen Bates, "New Mission for Man of Many Talents" *Guardian Unlimited/Special reports*, July 24, 2002 (Downloaded September 12, 2002). Available from http:www.guardian.co.uk/religion/Story/0,2673,762065,00.html.

1

of membership in the southern hemisphere indicates a major shift in power and authority. This very well may be a key reason an outsider was chosen as Archbishop of Canterbury: to show the world wide Communion that Anglicanism, though English in origin and perspective, is now ready to change.[2]

Aged 52 at the time of his selection, Rowan Douglas Williams is the youngest man to be appointed Archbishop of Canterbury since Charles Manners in 1805. He could remain in this position for the better part of the next two decades which would be easily long enough to set the tone for all of the twenty-first century.

He is the first Archbishop in one hundred twenty years (since E. W. Benson) to bring school-aged children to Lambeth palace.[3] He has never been a rector or vicar of a parish, serving his entire career as an academic until his appointment as bishop of Monmouth in 1992.

Williams was born June 14, 1950 in Swansea to a Welsh-speaking family of the modest middle class. His family worshiped initially at a local Presbyterian Church, before being drawn to an Anglo-Catholic parish some distance away. It was here, All Saints, Oystermouth, that the teenage Williams came under the influence of a mentor, Canon Eddie Hughes, who remained a friend and confidant for the next thirty years.[4]

From Dynevor Secondary School, Williams went on to Christ College, Cambridge, to study theology. He is an accomplished academic theologian, with a deep sense of social concern, especially for the plight of the poor. In a well documented story, Williams was standing in line at a commencement service at Oxford to receive his doctorate, when a nearby tramp summoned him for assistance. Williams left the line, walked over to the man and began talking to him, finally telling him that he was busy, but promised to meet him later, which he did.[5]

His academic rise was meteoric: Cambridge for his bachelors (1971) and masters (1975), Oxford for his doctorate in Russian Orthodox Theology (1975), then on to be tutor at Westcott House Cambridge (1977-1980), eventually becoming lecturer in Divinity at Cambridge (1980-1986) and Dean and Chaplain at Clare College, Cambridge (1984-1986). At age 36 he was appointed Lady Margaret Professor of Divinity at Oxford (1986-1992). Six years later, at age 42, he became Bishop of Monmouth. In 1998, Williams was considered for bishop of the south London diocese of Southwark, but a sharp rift developed between then Archbishop of Canterbury George Carey and Williams about gay and lesbian issues. When Carey asked if Williams would "toe the line"[6] and promise not to ordain non-celibate gays or lesbians, Williams emphatically stated that he could not make such a promise.[7] This response caused his consequent removal from consideration. Two years later, the "disestablished"

---

[2]Ibid.
[3]Ibid.
[4]Ibid
[5]Ibid.
[6]Ibid.
[7]Ibid.

church of Wales elected him to be Archbishop.

Even with his hectic schedule as a diocesan and then archbishop, Williams has kept writing. Many find that his books are often brilliant, yet profoundly subtle. This subtlety makes his writings ponderous and difficult to read. One British reporter describes him as being "so vague he could get lost taking his dog for a walk."[8] In addition to his often brilliant concepts, it is the style of his writings that gives insight into the man. With closer scrutiny, one discovers that Williams is a master of the passive voice, seldom making bold black and white statements. Instead he regularly uses terms like "it seems" or "a possible answer" and so forth.

He seems fascinated with the obtuse and obscure. It is with a nonconfrontational style that he makes his points in ways that generally do not offend or annoy (with notable exceptions,) even about controversial social issues, such as the war in Iraq or human sexuality. He does this primarily because he challenges the issue and not the person advocating a position. He always remains civil and courteous in his writings.

Upon further examination, it becomes clear that Williams is one of those curious admixtures of orthodox and *avant garde.* His book topics range from "icons" to "ethics." His *magnum opus* refutes the heretical charges against Arius, the fourth century cleric whose views prompted the calling of the first ecumenical council of Nicea in 325 AD and the consequent council of Constantinople in 381 AD. Out of these two councils came the creed that states that Jesus is indeed "true God from true God." To defend Arius against orthodox claims is tantamount to defending Judas Iscariot, which Williams cheerfully acknowledges.[9] This speaks to his tendency to be an advocate for the underdog, especially in sociological matters. His abiding premise is that he does not want to shut down discussion prematurely.

A self-described "hairy lefty,"[10] Williams looks more the part of an eccentric academic than a sophisticated, urbane Archbishop of Canterbury. He is married to fellow theologian Jane Williams and together they have two children, Rhiannon and Pip. By most accounts, Williams is not a strong administrator, so he gathers around him people whom he knows and trusts to do much of the day to day managing.[11]

British reporter Graham Turner of *The Daily Telegraph* states that Williams is a genuinely profound man who is "modest and humorous; a poet who has his spiritual feet on the ground; a compassionate man who is particularly good at helping lame dogs who can no longer climb over stiles." Turner goes on to say that Williams is a skilled mediator between conflicting parties, but "he is hopeless at formulating strategy."[12] Even those with significant theological differences agree that Williams is a gifted reconciler. "One of his great achievements has been to help church people of

---

[8]Alex Kirby, "The Challenges facing the New Archbishop" *BBC News/UK,* July 23, 2002, downloaded October 4, 2002 from http://news.co.uk./1/hi/uk/213088.stm.

[9]Rowan Williams, *Arius: Heresy and Tradition* (Grand Rapids, Michigan: W.B.Eerdmans, 2001), 1.

[10]Bates.

[11]Ibid.

[12]Graham Turner, "Four Twists in a Canterbury Tale," *news telegraph.co.telegraph.co.us,* March 30, 2002. Downloaded November 4, 2002.

different persuasions to listen to each other" writes Paul Handley in the British newspaper *The Independent on Sunday.*[13]

Today, with significant pressure to break the unity of this very diverse communion, any Archbishop of Canterbury needs to be a gifted reconciler. He also needs a blend of wit and wisdom, righteousness and reason, restraint and forthrightness, piety and pragmatism, keenness and kindness. He must have a delicate blend of head and heart. Fortitude, both intestinal and intellectual, grounded in prayer and humor, must hold sway at even the most trying times. In other words, he must be "wise as a serpent and innocent as a dove."[14] Time and the Holy Spirit will tell if Rowan Williams can fill the bill. In the meantime, it is the intent of this thesis to show that he takes seriously the task of keeping the Anglican Communion together, and that with his considerable talents as a reconciler, he looks primarily to common experiences of the Gospel which empower divergent forces to accommodate their rather significant differences.

---

[13]Paul Handley, "The Patron Saint of Disruption" *The Independent on Sunday* December 1, 2002.

[14]Matthew 10:16 RSV.

CHAPTER II
THE CATHOLIC FAITH: THE MANIFESTATION OF COMMON EXPERIENCE AND ACCOMMODATION OF DIFFERENCES

To gain insight into Williams' emphasis on common experience and the accommodation of differences as foundational for unity in the Anglican Communion, one must examine his understanding of catholicity. Williams sees himself as a catholic and he refers to the catholic church as "the Church of catholic persons, listening patiently and expectantly to each other, and in this exchange being brought towards the truthfulness of Christ (judgment and promise), discovering more deeply the spring of their common life, how the one Christ appears in the real diversity of many lives."[1] He believes that to live out the catholic faith is often daunting because there is always the tendency to indulge in "lazy and arbitrary individualism" on the one hand or to embrace the "abstract generalities of moral systems" on the other.[2] To stay open and listen is the catholic task.

To better understand his concept of the catholic faith, it is helpful to look at some of his writings on the topic. In an article he wrote in *The Oxford Companion to Christian Thought* entitled "Catholicity,"[3] Williams presents the definition of "catholic" given by Cyril of Alexandria, a fourth century bishop.[4] Williams notes that Cyril offers five components which comprise the catholic faith:

---

[1] Rowan Williams "Teaching the Truth" in *Living Tradition: Affirming Catholicism in the Anglican Church*, ed. Jeffrey John (Boston: Cowley Publications, 1992) 41.
[2] Ibid.
[3] Rowan Williams, "Catholicity," in *The Oxford Companion to Christian Thought*, ed. Adrian Hastings, Alistair Mason and Hugh Pyper (Oxford: Oxford University Press, 2000), 102.
[4] This is from Cyril's eighteenth lecture to the catechumens.

1. It is found *everywhere*: it isn't the religion of one race or group.
2. It teaches the *whole* truth, all that people need to know for their salvation.
3. It makes holiness possible for *all* kinds of people, rich and poor, clever and simple.
4. It faces and deals with *all* the sickness and sins of human beings.
5. And it displays the fullest possible *variety* of human excellence and every kind of spiritual gift.[5]

These concepts are imperative. Common experiences of the faith are found everywhere, the accumulation of these experiences is the means of teaching all that is needed for salvation; all kinds of people need to share their experiences and in so doing all the sickness and sins of the human condition are addressed. For the church to be fully catholic or unified, the fullest variety of experiences and spiritual gifts are to be accommodated as a common experience of the Gospel.

In an article entitled, "Teaching the Truth" in *Living Tradition: Affirming Catholicism in the Anglican Church*, Williams goes on to affirm Cyril's definition, that "catholic" has to do with the whole rather than the part.[6] He extrapolates Cyril's position to emphasize two points: the first is to tell the *whole truth about God.* [7] This means that the catholic faith tells the truth of God concerning all that which is "visible and invisible."[8] The catholic faith holds nothing back for any special individual or group. The catholic faith is to bring about "healing" for all that ails body, mind or spirit.[9] The catholic faith proclaims a God who is not "jealous of creation or self-protective."[10] The catholic faith celebrates a God who through inconceivable love is "generous without reserve and dependable without change."[11] This is the God who "holds nothing back," who gave his all in Christ Jesus.

However, to encounter "the whole truth of God" can be "chaotic."[12] Williams gives the example of Pentecost and the resultant "outbreak of baffling, noisy, exuberant talk in diverse languages."[13] In this chaotic experience, God ironically communicates with people who heretofore have not been included in His divine inclusiveness. Throughout church history, in times of renewal from Pentecost through the Reformation, on to various revivals, there have been "new words for praying and singing... [in which event all people, clergy and laity alike have the] authority to talk *of* God and *to* God."[14] This is important "because to be God is to be the generosity of

---

[5]"Teaching the Truth," 29-30.
[6]Ibid., 30.
[7]Ibid.
[8]Ibid
[9]Ibid.
[10]Ibid.
[11]Ibid, 31.
[12]Ibid.
[13]Ibid.
[14]Ibid.

self-communication"[15] to people who often, are slow to understand. God will use chaotic disorder to bring more people to "the whole truth about God."

Williams uses this as foundation for what he calls "Catholic talk," which he describes as openness to all the ways that God chooses to speak to and through the most unusual people.[16] He states that conversation about God, even teaching about God is not limited to those in formal positions of authority. This is important because there is an endemic clericalism among self-identified Catholics which manifests itself as an unhealthy deference to those who are ordained, simply because they are ordained. God speaks to and through all the baptized, not just to those in holy orders.[17] The language of the catholic faith is radically inclusive. For example, the common factor in all the debate about various heresies of the first few centuries of the church is what Williams believes is based on a "single vision," a limited vision "of the God who holds nothing back."[18] For Williams, this is expressed in the tension between the limited conventional "language of creed and worship" over against modern pronouncements, especially scientific and cultural pronouncements, which seem to contradict or refute elements of faith: for instance accounts of Creation, the Incarnation, the Trinity and so forth.[19]

This cuts several different ways. Not only does it apply to conservative orthodox Christians, who revere the traditional language and extrapolations of the faith over against what they perceive as encroachment of the world, but it also applies to liberals who exhibit their own "tight orthodoxy, in their concern that people will be made anxious by complexities or by pressure to accept the incomprehensible."[20] It is at this point that he offers three warnings:

1. "First beware of being sentimental about simplicity." Sentimentality about simplicity is seductive. On the one hand, there needs to be a constant awareness of the need to strip away pretense, to get to the core, foundational elements of the faith. On the other hand, there are constant temptations to take short cuts and to come up with pithy clichés that are just too simplistic. It is easy to sentimentalize a simple answer to a very complex problem. For example, the liberal response to difficult issues often tends to be a longing for more loving or accepting actions and attitudes. If that were to occur, then all difficulties would be abolished. This is naive. Orthodox conservatives, in contrast, tend to look to their own simplistic answers: "if only they were more faithful and self disciplined in saying their prayers, [in submitting to scripture] or coming to Mass, then all would be well."[21]

2. "Secondly, beware of patronizing." It is easy to fall into a patronizing attitude if one believes that he or she has the "truth" and the opposing side does not. The

---

[15]Ibid.
[16]Ibid., 31-32.
[17]Ibid.
[18]Ibid.
[19]Ibid.
[20]Ibid., 33.
[21]Ibid.

assumption is that there is only one manifestation of the truth and truth transcends "thoughtful uncertainty."[22] A patronizing attitude unchecked can soon become condescending and that in turn can lead to hubris, which is the polar opposite of the humble attitude of a servant.

3. Know that "doctrine can be pressed into the service of inhuman and unchristian oppression."[23] From the Crusades to the inquisition of heretics, to those who commit sexual sins, or are the victims of such sins today, the church has sometimes been cruel both to her own members and to those outside the faith in the name of correct doctrine. Again it is ironic that doctrinal truth can be the means of oppression. God's truth is most disarming often when it is least articulate. Williams believes strongly that telling God's truth not only disarms, it also fully and truly liberates. Again, the irony is that God's truth "disorients us, by the recovery of whatever it was that on Easter morning sent the first witnesses of the resurrection away afraid to speak...we are desperately in need of something—in our culture, in our individual experience— that makes us inarticulate."[24] Williams gives an outline describing this kind of inarticulation:

- *Tell me about God*
- *Watch*
- *What does the doctrine of the Trinity mean?*
- *Watch*
- *Why should I confess Jesus as Lord?*
- *Watch*[25]

It is in these times of watchful silence, while waiting for articulation of the incredible, life-giving aspects of the Gospel, that the truth of God is manifested most powerfully.

It is from here that Williams moves to the second part of his article: "*telling the truth about humanity.*"[26] Williams refers to Paul as he emphasizes that there is one Gospel for all people, but there is not one single formula for presenting the Gospel. He gives two reasons: "The first is that we are not in control of where people are."[27] This is in terms of geography, culture and psychology. People have histories, cultures, pain, pleasure, families, and jobs. Sometimes in the midst of crisis, for example, silence is the best way to convey the Good News of Jesus. The one wishing to share the Gospel may do so most effectively by being a contemplative presence at the moment of pain. It is in this silence that the truth of God can be most eloquent.

---

[22]Ibid., The author is reminded of a saying his father, a professor of agriculture at the University of Idaho, used to say:
"Education moves one from cocksure ignorance to thoughtful uncertainty."
[23]Ibid.
[24]Ibid., 35.
[25]Ibid, 36.
[26]Ibid.
[27]Ibid.

"A second point....you cannot articulate a moral and Christian judgment by speaking in a way in which you could not speak if the object of your judgment were actually *there*."[28] Williams is referring less to gossip and more to the understanding of reality that different cultures experience. The catholic faith is for all people in all times in all places, but "the most uncatholic thing we can do is to tailor what we say for a limited range of people...."[29] The challenge is to keep the vocabulary of faith while striving to speak the language of those to and for whom the message is intended.[30] Again Williams observes that often the most effective witness is silence. The words of the Psalmist ring true: "Be still and know that I am God."[31]

Rupert Shortt, in his book *Rowan Williams: An Introduction,* conveys Williams' thoughts on the tension of catholic communication this way: "Say too little, and you may betray the costly demands of the gospel. Say too much, and you risk sounding fanciful or authoritarian."[32] Effectiveness in being communicative is always the goal.

Williams explains further about the importance of being "communicative" for the catholic faith:

> This is what I mean by the *'communicative'*: a theology experimenting with the rhetoric of its uncommitted environment...The assumption is that this or that intellectual idiom not only offers a way into fruitful conversation with the current environment but also that the unfamiliar idiom may uncover aspects of the deposit of belief hitherto unexamined. In fact, it involves a considerable act of trust in the theological tradition, a confidence that the fundamental categories of belief are robust enough to survive the drastic experience of immersion in other ways of constructing and construing the world.[33]

He is saying that this communicative view must be firmly based on the sound trust of the fundamental categories of the faith, so that it empowers confidence to encounter other world views and not be threatened.

Williams goes on to maintain that the language of the faith needs to experiment with the uncommitted environment, often in such ways that are beyond the standard means and mode of communication, but are necessary if the gospel is to be heard by those who regularly tune it out. It takes robust belief to endure, let alone engender, this kind of communication. Usually this is the role of the professional theologian,

---

[28]Ibid., 37.

[29]Ibid., 38.

[30]This is a challenge that Bible translators constantly face. Dr. Michael Bollenbaugh, professor of Philosophy and Ethics at Northwest Christian College in Eugene, Oregon, tells the story of Wycliff missionaries in South America who were translating the Bible into the language of a particular tribe. These people were familiar with animal sacrifice, but knew nothing of sheep. The decision was to translate John 1:29 as "Behold, the chicken of God who takes away the sin of the world."

[31]Psalm 46:10 RSV

[32]Rupert Shortt, *Rowan Williams: An Introduction* (London: Darton-Longman-Todd, 2003), 5.

[33]Rowen Williams, *On Christian Theology* (Oxford:Blackwell Publishers Ltd., 2000), xiv.

the one who has the time and training and inclination to think in such ways and to devise the means to bring about this communication.

Moving on, Williams writes in the prologue to his extensive collection of essays entitled, *On Christian Theology,* that there are two other distinctive functions of the catholic faith besides the "communicative." They are the "celebratory" and the "critical."[34] The celebratory component of the church is chiefly liturgical: sermons and hymns celebrate the life of Christ; a priest "celebrates" the Eucharist. Celebrations tend "to evoke a fullness of vision" rather than to establish systematic argument for the faith.[35] The celebratory aspect of the faith focuses on the "doing" of theology, especially the mysteries of the faith. Williams notes that it is the celebratory aspects of the faith which "hint at the gratuitous mysteriousness of what theology deals with, the sense of a language trying unsuccessfully to keep up with a datum that is in excess of any foresight, any imagined comprehensive structure."[36] His third area is the "critical." Rupert Shortt observes that for Williams "Critical theology focuses on the awkward questions."[37] Whether it is human sexuality, ecumenical relations, or issues of peace and justice, critical theology always address difficult areas, not so much to come up with answers, but rather to acknowledge the hopelessness of the human condition without the beneficial presence of grace. It is here that Williams affirms that under girding all three aspects of the catholic faith, the communicative, the celebratory and the critical, is the need for "the inescapable place of repentance in all theological speech worth the name."[38] Williams writes:"There is no Catholic discipleship without repentance: we are brought to Jesus Christ for judgment and for healing; we are to be shown uncomfortable truths."[39] The constant pull of sin, the world, the flesh and the devil would draw the catholic (in fact all Christians) away from God's constant yearning and effort to be made known and to bring love to a broken world. Repentance is more than being sorry: it is the constant course check of those wishing to be faithful and then trusting in God's grace.

In review, for Williams, common experience and the accommodation of differences are foundational for unity, and this is manifested as the "catholic"faith. This catholic faith tells the whole truth about God, who holds nothing back, who gives His all in Christ Jesus. It tells the truth about humanity. This catholic faith is implemented in three ways: the communicative, the celebratory and the critical. The communicative task is to convey this truth, the celebratory task is the "doing" of this truth, and the critical task is to ask difficult, often awkward questions about divine and human truth. There often will not be one immediate answer, but the ongoing task is for the various members to stay open and listen to one another and for the voice of God in all its forms.

---

[34]Ibid., xiii.
[35]Ibid., xiv.
[36]Ibid., xv.
[37]Shortt, 6-7.
[38]*On Christian Theology*, xvi.
[39]*Living Tradition*, 40.

CHAPTER III

WILLIAMS' VIEW OF THE HISTORIC DEVELOPMENT OF THE CATHOLIC FAITH FROM THE APOSTLES THROUGH THE CONFLICT WITH ARIUS

The debate about catholicity over the centuries "came to be dominated by issues of order and sacramental validity, rather than the limits of the true catholic *faith.*" [1] This is true, especially, in the recent conversations between Anglicans and Roman Catholics. Much of this interchange has focused on the question of authority, which in turn has led to sharp exchanges about the legitimacy of various ordained offices. Williams argues that the catholic faith has to do with "the living truth about God rather than something capable of institutional checking or validating." [2] He notes that current thought about catholicity is moving toward a growing sense of "wholeness or integrity of faith." [3]

Williams believes that there needs to be a return to the understanding of the primitive church which appealed "to common *experience*" [4] as the unifying factor of the faith even as these early Christians tried to come to terms with "a set of competing claims" [5] about the crucified and risen Lord Jesus. Early Christians either accommodated each other because, with few exceptions, they spent more time trying to stay alive and evangelizing than they did in engaging in sophisticated dialogue about the nature of God. Williams thinks that this appeal to common experience and the accommodation of differences was the norm in the primitive church; it has been the underlying foundation for the church through the centuries, and it needs to be reemphasized today.

Williams turns to the history of the primitive church and writes about a wide and very diverse group of people who had very different perspectives on the faith. [6] He

---

[1] *The Oxford Companion to Christian Thought,* 103.
[2] Ibid.
[3] Ibid.
[4] Rowan Williams, ed., *The Making of Orthodoxy: Essays in Honour of Henry Chadwick* (Cambridge: Cambridge University Press, 1989) 8. Today Charismatic/Pentecostal Christians use this as a primary understanding of orthodoxy.
[5] Ibid. 2.
[6] Rowan Williams, *The Wound of Knowledge: A Theological History from the New Testament to Luther and St. John of the Cross* (Eugene, OR: Wipf & Stock Publishers, 1998).

refers to this as the "ways in which a succession of saints attempted to articulate their vision of the Christian calling."[7] The story of each person begins with an account of how sin is forgiven by means of the cross of Christ.[8] In this they shared the common experience of the redeeming love of Jesus. Their accommodation of differences came about by the use of common language, in what became the New Testament, about the cross. Williams therefore begins with the New Testament and the cross of Christ, for "Without the cross, there would be no New Testament."[9] "Those who at first believed in Jesus of Nazareth, as the Messiah, had to resolve the appalling paradox that the fulfiller of God's Law had been condemned and killed by the people of God, under the law of God. The new age of the Messiah...had dawned in the slaughter of the Messiah at the instigation of the messianic people."[10] Realizing this, the people of God began looking for clear-cut answers. They turned to the Law, but as St. Paul points out (especially in Romans 9-11) the law ultimately is futile. It is the Law which caused the death of Jesus. For Williams, it is evident that the Law cannot save because it is "most fundamentally self-dependence."[11] Self-dependence comes as result of self-centeredness which is the "refusal of grace, of reconciliation."[12] At the core of the catholic faith are the transcendence of self and the affirmation of a community of faith under-girded by the hope of reconciliation in Christ, something which Christ always initiates and to which the community is called to respond. Williams writes "Self-dependence is the subtlest mechanism of self-destruction, and to cling to it in the face of grace is a thinly veiled self hatred."[13]

The hope and promise of the catholic faith is the Holy Spirit which supports and uplifts until all may see that the "veil of the Law is removed [and] illusion is stripped away."[14] This does not come easily, quickly nor permanently, but painfully "by means of the pervasive and inexorable experience of failure."[15] However, this failure, symbolized by the cross, brings new life. The catholic faith is living out this new life, which is not a possession, but literally New Life through the waters of Baptism.

Baptism is the means to new life for Christians. New life "implies movement and growth" and Williams asserts that "not to grow is to fall away."[16] Painfully, this post-baptismal growth usually comes about "by anguish, darkness and stripping."[17] This is a theme that is affirmed from St. Paul throughout the development of the church, and it must always be asserted that "God is *in* our pain and our protest."[18]

---

[7]Ibid., 2.
[8]Ibid.
[9]*The Wound of Knowledge*, 3.
[10]Ibid.
[11]Ibid., 6.
[12]Ibid.
[13]Ibid.
[14]Ibid.
[15]Ibid.
[16]Ibid., 8.
[17]Ibid., 10.
[18]Ibid., 11.

This is the stuff of suffering in which martyrs of the primitive church and martyrs today find common ground. (In a smaller way, it is also true for any faithful believer who bears witness to the suffering of Christ on the cross.) "There is a circle of interpretation, the martyr finds God in his suffering because he is assured that his Christian identity as a child of the Father, as a redeemed person, is the fruit of Christ's cross...[and] is filled out by the present experience of the martyr."[19] This suffering is not limited to individuals; it is also the suffering of accommodation in which seemingly conflicting experiences are not viewed as the common experience of the cross or even of resurrection, but as experiences which are incompatible with the catholic faith.

To counter this, Williams looks to post-biblical figures who were instrumental in the development of the catholic faith. He gives the example of the martyr Irenaeus of Lyons, who like the Apostle Paul, was primarily a letter writer, and as such, was not a systematic theologian.[20] A particular threat came to the church in the form of Gnosticism (a complex and subtle religion which used Christian language in the articulation of a position basically alien to the gospel.) In Gnosticism, "God and the world are strangers to one another: that there is a world is a result of accident or malevolence on the part of some heavenly power."[21] God doesn't love the world; at best He is apathetic toward it. Yet within it are divine souls which must escape the bondage of the material and the flesh. For the Gnostic, freedom is to escape via the means of transcending physical restraints. Gnostics viewed the Old Testament as an "embarrassment" because of "crude and superstitious beliefs about God's involvement with creation."[22] For the true Gnostic believer, God must be distant from the unpleasantness of human corruptibility. In refuting this, Irenaeus argued that God's love was expressed in becoming human and "sharing *in* what is human."[23] There is no strict separation of body and soul. God has acted in human history in the person of Jesus of Nazareth and thus cannot be separated from any human component including the body. Any savior that was disdainful of empathetic identification, and taught that the way to spiritual enlightenment was to purge or disregard the body, could have no sense of the history of God's redeeming work. This dualism of the body over against the soul was contrary to the Good News of the catholic faith. For in the catholic faith, God loves all human beings in their totality, fallen though they may be, and the Godhead functions still as the one who creates, redeems and sanctifies. This is not a select message, but one that is available to all. This view is foundational for a sense of accommodation.

Over a century later, the debate about how God came in the flesh became a watershed for the catholic faith. As background, the emperor Constantine issued the Edict of Milan in 313 AD, which allowed the Christian faith to be tolerated officially

---

[19]Ibid., 15.
[20]Ibid., 23.
[21]Ibid.
[22]Ibid., 26.
[23]Ibid., 28.

in the Roman Empire. No longer did Christians worry about Roman persecution. Instead they could use their energy to think systematically about the essence of the catholic faith. Things that had been overlooked for three centuries were now becoming issues of major conflict. One very important issue concerned the nature of Jesus. Was he *homoousion* (the same substance) or was he a similar but different substance, a creation of God? Although that was the primary public focus of the theological debate, Williams argues that it was more about political power and the refusal to be accommodating, and less about theology. A figure named Arius of Alexandria was to be the lightening rod for the conflict.

Williams makes clear that the person of Arius must be distinguished from "Arianism." "'Arianism' as a coherent system, founded by a single great figure and sustained by his disciples, is a fantasy...."[24] Historically, however, the church has been reluctant to agree with this. For example some of the vilification of Arius stemmed from military conflict years later. Many of the marauding Goths who sacked Rome were Arians and the victims in Rome personified their pain in the person of Arius whom they blamed for what they viewed as heretical atrocities of those pagan Goths.[25] Later on in the middle ages it was not uncommon to see Arius depicted alongside Judas Iscariot in Church art.[26] Williams emphasizes the distinction between Arius and Arianism and maintains that evidence shows that Arius got caught up in a power struggle with Alexander, the Bishop of Alexandria, and lost less for his theological views and more for his political incompetence. This is important because Williams argues that the views of Arius are not incompatible with the catholic faith.

Here are key reasons Williams suggests that are sufficient to affirm Arius's catholicity: First, he was a faithful exegete of scripture.[27] A pivotal passage for him was Proverbs 8:22 which states "The Lord created me at the beginning of his work, the first of the acts of old."[28] One can readily see that several other scriptures also may have been important in Arius's thinking. For example:

> John 17:3 "this is eternal life, that they may know the only true God, and Jesus Christ whom thou has sent"
> Acts 2:36 "God has made him both Lord and Christ"
> Colossians 1:15 "He is the image of the invisible God, the firstborn of all creation."[29]

Williams contends that reverence and devotion to scripture are necessary components of a catholic faith.

---

[24] *Arius*, 82.
[25] Ibid., 1.
[26] Ibid.
[27] Ibid., 107.
[28] RSV
[29] Other passages Arius may have used to develop his theological position were Ps.45:7-8; Ps.110:3; Is.1:2; Dt.32:18; Rom.11:36; Phil.2:9 etc.

Second, Williams contends that Arius was part of that great Judeo-Christian tradition which believes that God can do all things, including bridging the gap between the divine and the created order. God's will is sufficient to do all that God desires. He is contained by nothing: "he does not have to accommodate his will to independent co-eternal matter, nor is there any internal necessity generating a hierarchy of emanations from the primal purity of the divine life itself."[30] God can do what God wants to do, including making Himself present as something He created. Arius' intent was not to advance a provocative new doctrine: rather he was trying to clarify orthodox catholic doctrine.[31] It was experienced by the faithful and Arius was striving to articulate and clarify that common experience. In fact, Arius viewed himself as Trinitarian, especially in light of Matthew 28:19 where Jesus calls his disciples to baptize all nations "in the name of the Father and of the Son and of the Holy Spirit."[32]

Williams points out three basic theological points that Arius and his followers make:

i.   The Son is a creature, that is, a product of God's will;
ii   Son is therefore a *metaphor* for the second hypostasis, and therefore must be understood in the light of comparable usage in scripture;
iii. The Son's status, like his very existence, depends upon God's will.[33]

Williams notes that Arius was concerned about "loose ends" and his theology was at least striving to tie up those loose ends.[34] Key for Arius, Williams believes, was his understanding that God's will was more than sufficient to establish a creature as His son and that was a sufficient explanation for the 'sonship' of Jesus.

Williams' thesis is that the teachings of Arius and catholic were "coeval" (that is the same as or complimentary) in the fourth century church,[35] and that catholicity took on a legalistic view during that period which changed the very nature of the catholic faith and unity. Order became more important than either common experience or accommodation of differences. Under the Emperor, "Catholic unity could at least be enforced by law, the law of a (more or less) Christian ruler."[36] Order in the church became intertwined with order in the Empire. Or, to be more precise, disorder in the church was a threat to the empire. To promote this thesis, Williams turns his attention to the under-lying power vacuum that had developed in the fourth century church after the Edict of Milan.

As nature abhors a vacuum, so too does any institution that has unclear lines of authority, especially during times of stressful change. Experiences that are often viewed as subjective can be threatening when order is considered to be paramount. The

---

[30]*Arius*, 175.
[31]Ibid., 115.
[32]Ibid., 96.
[33]Ibid., 109.
[34]Ibid., 230.
[35]Ibid., 24.
[36]Ibid., 86.

struggle to clarify order and hence to fill this power vacuum came to a head. It was between local parishes and the diocese, collegial presbyters against the centralized authority of the bishop. The Arian conflict was largely about power. For example, tradition has it that an issue arose between Arius and Alexander, the local bishop of Alexandria, about the custodial privilege of the skeletal remains of the local patron saint, the blessed Mark, the apostle. Those in charge of these remains would have a position of power in the church and Arius was the custodian of the relics. Williams writes that if true, then this was "a fact that would have no doubt... [both] complicated his relations with the bishop and reinforced his prestige in the local church."[37] Alexander did not like it.

The tension between Arius and Alexander grew significantly in the restructuring of church order which became a conflict between an increasingly centralized authority of bishop over against local autonomy of priests and their congregations. Arius was not alone; he was just the most prominent. There were other presbyters in Alexandria "who were not docile diocesan clergy"[38] and did not like the increasing episcopal power. Arius became a spokesman for those who resisted the increasing power of the bishop. Alexander decided to flex his ecclesiastical muscles to consolidate his power.[39] There are indications that things got very personal very fast and he and Arius met head on. Williams notes that the two "publicly repudiated each other's theologies" prior to the issue of *homoousion*. The conflict over the nature of Jesus seems to have been more an occasion for censure then it was the cause of censure. Arius rallied sympathetic presbyters behind him and Alexander could have none of that. Eventually the power struggle grew so intense that a sharp rift was developing in the diocese (and one can assume elsewhere in the empire), a rift between "the collegial authority of presbyters," on the one hand, versus the increasingly centralized, top down authority of the diocesan bishop, on the other.[40] Williams sums it up: "The beginnings of Arianism lie, as much as anything in the struggles of the Alexandrian episcopate to control and unify a spectacularly fissiparous Christian body..."[41] This issue of authority was soon to be settled when the emperor Constantine called an ecumenical council to resolve the crisis. The conflict had become a threat to the unity of the empire and this was not to be tolerated.

The standard interpretation of the council of Nicea in 325 AD was that it intended to resolve the question of the true nature of Jesus. Although this was an integral part of the council, Williams argues that Nicea was also about centralized authority and enforced uniformity, rather than a unity based on experiences of grace and loving accommodation of differences. Prior to this state-mandated gathering of bishops, "relative pluralism, with a regular ritual focus, and an agreed set of texts as a basis for teaching and exploration, was appropriate to a church which lacked any notion of itself as a single

---

[37]Ibid., 43.
[38]Ibid., 44.
[39]Ibid., 45.
[40]Ibid.
[41]Ibid., 46.

COMMON EXPERIENCE
AND THE
ACCOMMODATION
OF
DIFFERENCES:

*THE FOUNDATION FOR UNITY IN
ROWAN WILLIAMS' VIEW OF THE CHURCH*

BRYCE McPROUD

Wipf & Stock Publishers
Eugene, Oregon

Wipf & Stock Publishers
199 West 8th Avenue, Suite 3
Eugene, OR 97401

10   9   8   7   6   5   4   3   2   1

institutional unit...[42] After the council, there was a much tighter and uniformed understanding of the catholic faith. Experience and accommodation were deemphasized.

Williams writes that "by the second decade of the fourth century the visible harmony and uniformity of the church had become...a question of public and legal interest... Catholic unity could be enforced by law."[43] He goes on to state that "the wrong sort of Christian group was regarded pretty much as the church itself had been regarded by the pagan empire, as something subversive to the sacred character of social life."[44]

In review, the catholic faith is about sharing the experience of the encounter with the crucified and risen Lord Jesus. From the time of the apostles, there has been an appeal to this common experience, even in the midst of competing claims about the nature of this encounter. It is evident that these different understandings were accommodated because these early Christians were focused on evangelizing and surviving in the face of terrible oppression.

The fourth century ushered in a time of safety of the church, but with it came power struggles of epic proportion, the most notable was between Arius and his Bishop, Alexander. Williams contends that this was a struggle more about enforced, even coercive order and less about theology. If the competing factions had been more charitable in sharing their common experience of grace and less about trying to defeat the other, Arius and his views would probably not received an official censure at the Council of Nicea.

When all is said and done, Williams maintains that Arius' views could very well have been catholic, and the political environment was more influential in his condemnation than was his theology. By implication, this kind of thinking is key to Williams' understanding of the catholic faith as an inclusive more than an exclusive faith today. A colleague of his, Bishop Richard Holloway wrote the following in the introduction to *Living Tradition: Affirming Catholicism in the Anglican Church.* It speaks to the general tenor of Williams' beliefs articulated in his evaluation of Arian conflict of the fourth century and to the conflict in the church today.

> "There is a strong schismatic energy at work in our church...The drive toward schism, the compulsion to create tidy, homogeneous ecclesiastical units of the usually angry and like-minded, is essentially anti-catholic and sectarian. The genius of Catholicism is not sameness, but universality, encompassability, the generosity that is inclusive, rather than the narrowness of spirit that is always looking for ways of locking people out."[45]

It is with this sense of universality, encompassability and generosity that Williams looks to prominent Christian thinkers following Arius up to Luther and St. John of the Cross, to examine how their common experience of the Gospel are models of accommodation for the church today.

---

[42]Ibid., 90.
[43]Ibid., 86.
[44]Ibid., 90-91.
[45]*Living Tradition*, 15.

CHAPTER IV

AN HISTORICAL PERSPECTIVE OF CATHOLICITY FROM AUGUSTINE AND PELAGIUS TO LUTHER AND ST. JOHN OF THE CROSS

Rowan Williams states that "Christianity is a set of competing claims about a certain definable cluster of issues."[1] These would include the Resurrection, Pentecost, Episcopal authority and so forth. What initially brought primitive Christians together was the "appeal to common experience"[2] which eventually needed some form of concrete expression, while allowing for conflicting ambiguity. This is the ongoing issue for the church today. Williams writes: "The 'catholic' insight is that [the church] continues to be *constituted* by historical mediations—gospel and canon, sacrament, succession, communion, debate and exchange, with all the ambiguities involved in the life of the historical and visible social realities, the problems and power and guilt and forgiveness."[3] Williams refers to this as "an interwoven plurality of perspectives."[4] What they do is bring together a "complicated and muddled bundle of experiences ... a theatre for God's creative work."[5] This ongoing "theatre" from Arius to Luther is the focus of this chapter. It is a chosen cast of characters who demonstrate often conflicting perspectives on the reality of their common experience of God in Christ, the power of the cross and the power of the Holy Spirit.

The purpose of studying these actors in history is to show the incredible mystery

---

[1] *Orthodoxy*, 2.
[2] Ibid., 8.
[3] Ibid., 17.
[4] Ibid., 18.
[5] *Wound of Knowledge*, 2.

of the commonality of these saints who lived out their faith in such diverse manners.[6] Some were censured by the church, while others were embraced as being teachers of the truth of God. Williams is not inclined to see such sharp divisions among conflicting parties. Just as Williams defended Arius against the charges of heresy put against him, so too does he look to find ways to include others whom history has deemed to be heretics. In so doing, Williams sets the stage for his proposal that experiences of the faith are common, even with seemingly conflicting interpretations, and the catholic faith must always strive to accommodate rather than eliminate.

Augustine and Pelegius

As an example, Williams refers to the conflict between Augustine, one of the great defenders of orthodox understanding of original sin, and Pelagius, an English monk, commonly referred to as a heretic, who thought that the goodness and freedom of humans stemmed from their creation in the image of God, and hence were sinless at birth. Sin, for Pelagius, was not about a natural state of being, but only about things done and left undone. The sacrifice of Christ was little more than a wonderful example of selfless love, which Christians should emulate. Virtue and holiness were human responsibilities and one did not need divine intervention to overcome sin. Augustine refuted this and asserted that humans have inherited the sin of Adam and consequently are helpless to overcome sin by their own efforts. The depravity of the human condition required the ultimate sacrifice of Christ's death on the Cross. It alone was sufficient to overcome the onerous nature of human sin.

Between the worlds of Augustine and Pelaglus—now, as in the fifth century—is a very wide gulf. The Pelagian view is to see the world as difficult, but essentially capable of being overcome with sufficient goodness and love. It is a challenge for human beings to exercise and extend themselves, but their efforts can suffice. Williams writes that this is a "world in which heroism is possible, in which good causes can be believed in, improvement of self and others can be sought with a clear eye and a clean conscience. Guilt is a straightforward question of responsible and deliberate delinquency; virtue or responsible and deliberate obedience. There is always a right answer."[7]

Opposed to this is Augustine's view of the world as sinful and broken. "This world represents sheer human defeat. In a sense it has no heroes: it has tragic protagonists, whose motivation is too unclear for them to be credibly heroic. Even its busiest agents are victims. Moral or social improvement is clouded by the certainty of failure and regression; and guilt and virtue are elusive and ambivalent ideas. Responsible and deliberate choice is the least part of motivation, good or ill. There are seldom right answers."[8] Any and all efforts to achieve salvation on one's own merits are futile and doomed for frustration. Only the grace of God through the passion of Christ on the Cross can overcome the power of the fall and the effects of sin.

---

[6]Ibid., 3.
[7]Ibid., 84
[8]Ibid., 85.

19

For Williams, neither Pelagius nor Augustine has a complete understanding of the catholic faith. However he is particularly critical of Augustine. Williams writes: "The world is a world capable of crucifying it's own health and the cross remains a stark reminder that there is little to hope for here. However, to concentrate exclusively on the dark side of Augustine's universe is misleading: there is little enough of hopefulness in the world, yet only in the world, only with other men and women, do we *learn* hope, pity, joy, trust or love. It is knowing both their utter and intense reality and their doomed frailty that begins to suggest to us the perspective of authentic hope."[9]

Antony and the Desert Fathers

Moving on, an important perspective for the development of the catholic faith came from those who fled to the desert and away from "the world," to discover God's voice speaking to them in the wilderness. Williams looks to the desert fathers. Antony, the founder of the monastic movement, began his self-imposed retreat into the Egyptian desert in the mid-third century in reaction to the contamination of the Roman Empire.[10] Over the years other hermits followed him.

Each hermit chose to seek enlightenment by probing his (or her) personal "darkness, [the place of] ... interior horror of temptation and fantasy."[11] Staying in one's cell was the means of overcoming "boredom, sexual frustration, restlessness, unsatisfied desire" and so forth. Temptation was a constant, and to stay still and confront it was done by "praying for strength and resolve and not for deliverance."[12] Williams' critique of this early monasticism was that it tended toward "an apparent glorification of will at the expense of grace."[13] However, Williams writes: "primitive monasticism is on the side of grace if only because of the profound acceptance of *failure....*"[14]

Williams asserts that the primary gift of primitive monasticism was the realization that no growth can "occur without the ... stripping of illusion."[15] This was done drastically by individuals who realized that the fantasies from the unconscious caused separation from God. In the desert community, the appropriate position was to encourage individual development without egocentricity, when each member strove for faithfulness primarily in the service to others in the community. Even the most isolated hermit engaged in the interconnectedness of burden-sharing as a direct result of the "emptying of self." These hermits fought their own demons, yet they shared stories of faith, prayed with and for each other, and were regularly seeking connection in their isolated lives.

---

[9] Ibid.
[10] Ibid., 92.
[11] Ibid., 94.
[12] Ibid.
[13] Ibid., 95.
[14] Ibid., 95-96.
[15] Ibid., 98.

Benedict of Nursia and Bernard of Clairvaux

The desert ascetics were the inspiration for later monastic development, especially in the thought and work of Benedict of Nursia. In the post-Nicene church, catholicity had become more rigid. Benedict wanted to simplify the faith while establishing a fixed rule of life. His simple vows of poverty, chastity and obedience in a communal life of study, work, rest, food, prayer and worship became the model for Western monasticism. Each community was based on Benedict's *Rule* and local custom.[16] In the eleventh century a reform movement arose, the Cistercians, which treated the *"Rule...*as a constitution or law book."[17] This strict interpretation provided a renewed simplicity for the monks, and it drew "uneducated" people to the movement.[18] One of these was a "maddeningly complex man," Bernard of Clairvaux, whom Williams describes as

> intolerant and unjust, sometimes politically unscrupulous, with an astonishing confidence in his own authority, and yet also loving and compassionate, reconciling, humble, bitterly aware of the oddity of his own position as a monk wielding vast influence in the world...Bernard was one of the great architects of medieval religious culture.[19]

Theologically, "Bernard compares the union of self and God with the mixing of water and wine and the heating of iron in fire."[20] This is accomplished through obedience to the church which is, according to Bernard, the only means of union with God. One's attitude in obedience must be motivated by the "humility of love" which is shown in the denial of self.[21] Even a rigid figure like Bernard has an important place in Williams understanding of an inclusive church. Bernard's story, though often fierce and violent, is a story of loyalty and conviction. Although Williams may very well want to modify some of Bernard's teachings, there is no question of his loyalty to the catholic faith and therefore Williams affirms his place in the church. If the catholic faith is to be encompassing, it must make room for troubling figures like Bernard, who was one of the great architects of medieval religious culture.

Thomas Aquinas and Meister Eckhart

Williams sharply criticizes the seminal work of Thomas Aquinas, perhaps the most influential Roman Catholic theologian of the Middle Ages. "It is often remarked that Aquinas manages to discuss subjects such as grace, contemplation and knowledge of God without any reference to Christ..."[22] The person of Christ is central for

---

[16]Ibid., 106
[17]Ibid., 107.
[18]Ibid.
[19]Ibid.
[20]Ibid., 111.
[21]Ibid., 113-114.
[22]Ibid., 124.

Williams, and any who would embrace the unity of the catholic faith must first and foremost acknowledge allegiance to the Lordship of Jesus. Williams does point out however, that Aquinas taught that grace was part of the Incarnation, and was therefore available to all, Christian or not. This is in accord with Williams own thinking,[23] and it is important because the church, as the Body of Christ, is not the sole recipient of God's grace.

In comparison, Williams seems to have a special fondness for Meister Eckhart, one of the disciples of Aquinas and a fellow Dominican. Eckhart was the subject of much controversy. Williams writes:

> Eckhart is at least as much poet as metaphysician—perhaps all the better a metaphysician for being a poet. In depth and imagination, he stands alone among his theological and philosophical contemporaries; the condemnation of his thinking came from far smaller souls than his own.[24]

Williams seems particularly drawn to Eckhart's depiction of "ecstasy," not as

> abnormal spiritual experience but the ecstasy of understanding, the transition of subject into object, the setting aside of self in order to let the observed and understood reality act without impediment. The self when made naked and poor is free to go forward to God and be welcomed into God."[25]

Eckhart's problem was that the catholic church of the fourteenth century had insufficient vocabulary "to express theologically the basic principles of its life, *ekstatsis*, emptying, displacement of sin in response to the self-emptying love of God, communion of God and, humanity by the presence of each in the other."[26] This is crucial for Williams. It is this giving up of "self" which is always needed, and which overcomes rigid external regulations, and which allows the church to be flexible and accommodating for divergent views.

Nominalism

Williams next reflects on the period of the late Middle Ages at which time there was "an increasing rationalism," not the hearty open rationalism of the renaissance, but pessimistic rationalism known as "nominalism."[27] Briefly, this was a system of thought which taught that entities like tree, stone, human, etc. do not have real existence in themselves and their names are purely a matter of "convention."[28] "There could be no certain (that is, experiential) knowledge of realities outside the realm of

---

[23] Ibid.
[24] Ibid., 135.
[25] Ibid.
[26] Ibid., 137.
[27] Ibid., 138.
[28] Ibid.

sense experience."[29] Therefore, any personal religious or spiritual knowledge was impossible. There were only two possibilities: one was that faith was "exclusively a matter of will," or somehow faith miraculously came to the Church as "authoritative dogma."[30] The connection between the two is a "willed...obedience to the Church's authority."[31] Therefore faith and will are interconnected, a position developed by the fourteenth century Franciscan Duns Scotus "for whom knowledge of God is essentially the willed human response to God's willed self-disclosure: will rather than understanding ...determines faith."[32]

Another Franciscan, William of Ockham developed this theme by pointing out that the doctrine of the Holy Trinity (and others) cannot be supported on rational grounds, but can be accepted by faith through the will as a "revealed" proposition of the Church.[33] The creation of the world by God *ex nihilo* (out of nothing), the freedom of the will and the primacy of humans created in the image of God, were foundational to his thought. "The equivalence of faith, knowledge and will serves to render belief invulnerable, at the cost of making it finally incommunicable."[34] Later, through the teaching of Gabriel Biel, nominalism was influential on the thought of Martin Luther, and hence the Reformation. It is this connection that makes nominalism important to Williams.

Luther and St. John of the Cross

Luther and the reformation changed the western world. As Williams notes, Luther emphasized "rediscovery of Scripture and the primitive tradition: he read Paul and Augustine for himself."[35] He was an advocate of *"Interpreting"* the Bible and the early Fathers, rather than analyzing them as did those of the scholastic school.[36] Luther's approach was to understand the relationship between natural "fact and transcending saving truth."[37] However, this was not a clean, crisp process. In the midst of his intellectual pursuits, he was wracked with guilt by his own shortcomings and he struggled to find how to please God. His torment was overwhelming. Williams states that

> Luther is a reminder to [all believers] that the strength of Christianity is its refusal to tune away from the central and unpalatable facts of human self-destructiveness; that it is there, the bitterest places of alienation, and that the depth and scope of Christ's victory can be tasted, and the secret joy which

---

[29]Ibid.
[30]Ibid.
[31]Ibid.
[32]Ibid., 139.
[33]Ibid.
[34]Ibid., 142.
[35]Ibid.
[36]Ibid., 142-143.
[37]Ibid., 142.

transforms all experience from within can come to birth, the hidden all-pervading liberation.[38]

Williams believes that Luther's message was that an overly rigid insistence on order and agreement will inevitably cause a reaction. If the requirement for order and agreement are too tight, reformers will emerge from the community who will challenge and even bring about schism if their understanding of a common experience is not accommodated. Luther is but one such figure.

Williams makes a curious comparison between Luther and the Reformation and the Spanish Carmelite, John of the Cross, and the Roman Catholic renewal of the sixteenth century. Spain was the European country least affected by the Reformation. It was still swaggering from its victories in the wars with Islam, and it was hungrily embarking on an expanded colonial empire. There was unrest, however, in some of the individuals of the monastic communities of the Spanish Church. Most prominent, perhaps, was St. John of the Cross, whose personal torment was parallel to Luther's "though neither would have relished the comparison."[39] Williams points out, (as with Luther) it is not possible to understand John without knowing of his torment, especially his time in prison as a result of the conflict between the reforming and conservative wings of his Carmelite order. His mental anguish was an experience of grace. John affirmed that grace overcomes the humdrum as well as the crisis, when the soul is bored as well as sorely tried. The Christian must surrender to grace, so one can have the hope of finding union with God.

> John sees clearly that the more we advance, the more matters will present themselves to us in these terms of choice for or against God—the almost harmless attachments to places and things, habits that are not gravely sinful, but are still selfish. These if neglected, will eventually be obstacles as great as any deliberate sin. [40]

John calls for testing the soul's true conversion which is voiced in the fervent prayer to God, "What do your really want?"[41] Reminiscent of Bonhoeffer's sense of "cheap grace," Williams notes, "If human desire is met with cheap and momentary gratifications, its proper transcendent directedness is threatened, if not negated."[42] Submitting to grace is neither cheap nor easy. It's hard and painful to purge oneself of the senses, that is, the manifestation of the self which is dominated "by physical desire and preference."[43] Williams notes John's two step process. First, the "night of the senses"

---

[38] Ibid., 158.
[39] Ibid., 159. John died alienated from his Carmelite order and is still not considered mainstream in the spirituality of the Roman Church. Ibid., 160.
[40] Ibid., 165.
[41] Ibid.
[42] Ibid., 166.
[43] Ibid.

in which there is the denial of the conscious self, and then there is the

> 'night of the spirit'[which] is a deeper and more bitter experience, striking
> harder at the very roots of illusion and systematically reducing human spiri-
> tual activity to the one act of faith and longing.[44]

John embraces the classic scholastic understanding of the three-fold aspects of the
soul —intellect, memory and love which must be purified if the offering of self is to
be complete. His position in the church, although controversial, is important for Williams because of his great emphasis on the denial of self.

In review, all of the aforementioned cast of characters (and many more) indicate
the great plurality of perspectives that make up the body of Christ. They are important for their personal faith, for the sharing of their stories, for the diversity of their
opinions and the representation of the very broad spectrum of the church. Williams
writes:

> Christianity begins in contradictions, the painful effort to live with the baf-
> fling plurality and diversity of God's manifested life—law and gospel,
> judgment and grace, the crucified Son crying to the Father. Christian expe-
> rience does not simply move from one level to the next and stay there, but is
> drawn again and again to the central fruitful darkness of the cross. But in
> this constant movement outwards in affirmation and inwards to emptiness,
> there *is* life and growth. The end is not yet; the frustrated longing for home-
> coming, for journey's end is unavoidable. Yet we can perhaps begin to see,
> through all the cost and difficulty, how we are entering more deeply into a
> divine life which is itself diverse and moving—Father and Son eternally
> brought to each other in Spirit. To discover in our 'emptying' and crucifying
> the 'emptying' of Jesus on the cross is to find God... [45]

For Williams there is the need for a twofold process. First there must be a constant awareness that Christ continually empties Himself on our behalf in an ongoing
act of selfless love. In response to this, Christians are called to empty themselves of
"self." When these are done in concert, then it is possible to accommodate the great
diversity of the church. From the time of the Apostles, there has been a struggle to
validate common experiences in a spirit of accommodation, knowing that with God
all things will be revealed on the last day. Until then, the mystery of the faith will be
manifested in the mystery of plurality and diversity.

---

[44]Ibid.
[45]Ibid., 178.

CHAPTER V

SACRAMENTAL COHESION: BAPTISM AND THE HOLY EUCHARIST

Williams believes that participating in the sacraments, especially Baptism and the Eucharist, is the concrete expression of common experience for Christians and it is therefore the means by which accommodation of differences is most easily accommodated in the church. The experience may have different interpretations, but it is universally acknowledged by Catholics as an affirmation of the work of Jesus. Williams sees "baptism as essentially a mark of individual confession.... [and] the Eucharist as a celebration of achieved local human fellowship."[1] He writes:

> How remarkable and unheard-of that bread should turn into flesh, that water should wash away sins! How doubly remarkable that the power to effect this should be mediated through frail earthen vessels (clergy)!"[2]

He muses that the most remarkable component of the sacramental mystery is the "uniqueness of Jesus Christ in his dying and rising."[3] This mystery is a source of grace and power for the church, and both sacraments affirm the Lordship of Jesus by his committed disciples. They are acts of obedience to Jesus Christ. They are acts of openness by the faithful so that they might be "converting signs of Jesus himself... [they are models] of receiving, not independent assaults on God by alienated, distant creatures. [Sacramental] signs are what Christ creates - his own self as gift."[4]

Williams asserts that the emphasis should be on what he calls "sacramental ac-

---

[1] *On Christian Theology,* 221.
[2] Ibid., 197
[3] Ibid.
[4] Ibid., 206.

tions," rather than on the objects of the sacramental action.[5] Sacramental action, the process of celebrating a sacrament, affirms the presence of the living Christ who is proclaimed and experienced in the community of believers. The purpose of sacraments is to reaffirm and strengthen that relationship with Christ and other believers. Williams writes that sacramental action moves the community from one kind of reality to another. He describes the transition this way:

> [There is] a pre-sacramental state, a secular or profane condition now imagined for ritual purposes, in the light of and in the terms of the transformation that is to be enacted; it tells us where we habitually are is not, after all, a neutral place but a place of loss or need. It then requires us to set aside this damaged or needy condition, so that in dispossessing ourselves of it we are able to become possessed operation like other kinds of social identity. The rite requires us *not* to belong anymore to the categories we thought we belonged in, so that a distinctive kind of new belonging can be realized. When this transition takes place, the presence and the power of the sacred is believed to be at work.[6]

Williams goes on to state that these sacramental actions are depictions of "a process of estrangement, surrender and re-creation."[7] Baptism is the means of inclusion and the Eucharist is the means of nurturing those who are members of the community.

Baptism is the culmination of missionary activity. Williams refers to the Great Commission from the Gospel of Matthew[8] at which time Jesus commands His disciples to baptize all nations in the name of the three persons of the Trinity. He writes:

> The Christian movement, as far back as we can trace it, is a *missionary* movement: that is, it works on the assumption that it has something to say that is communicable beyond its present boundaries and is humanly attractive or compelling across these boundaries. It assumes that it has the capacity and the obligation to seek to persuade persons from all imaginable human backgrounds that it is decisively relevant to their humanity, that it can deliver from whatever bondage women and men may happen to live under. Its relevance to all *depends* on its difference from existing patterns of human relation and power: if it 'fulfils' anything, it is a buried capacity for communion between human beings as such—as flesh and spirit, as mortal, sinful and walled-off from each other, in need of a relation God alone can provide. The Church is authorized to bring people into this unconstrained relation with God and each other through its participation in the authority of Jesus raised from the dead: the Risen One who is Lord of the Church is the one

---

[5] Ibid., 209.
[6] Ibid.
[7] Ibid., 210.
[8] Matthew 28:16-20.

rejected by the existing patterns of human corporate life, dying alone, so that his new life beyond death 'belongs' to none of those patterns.[9]

This implies that the power and presence of the crucified and risen Christ is manifested in the baptismal community in which there is a twofold ramification:
1. The individual receives new life in Christ
2. There is entrance into the communal life of the Body of Christ by sharing in his death.

Williams writes, "The pivotal point is this: death is normally a drastic severing of relations, death *isolates;* for Jesus, it's through death that a new and potentially infinite network of relations opens up."[10] It is in this new life in the community of those who share in Christ's Body that the importance of the Eucharist is emphasized.

The Eucharist recollects a complex event which has a twofold meaning. It is first to be interpreted as a sign of Jesus's death and its effects, while affirming that the death of Jesus is transformed as a life giving breaking and sharing of bread. The central transition here, as with baptism, is death presented as a passage into life. The wine poured out as shed blood is the mark of the covenant with the New Israel, the people of God. The movement is towards a declared commitment on God's part, sealed and assured by Jesus' death.

Williams observes the obvious: it is Jesus who makes Himself vulnerable and gives Himself over to those who would follow him, specifically His disciples. It is through this voluntary vulnerability that Jesus anticipates His betrayal. The Eucharistic liturgies of the church look to Paul, specifically in I Corinthians 11, to pinpoint "the night when He [Jesus] was betrayed."[11] This linkage between the betrayal of Jesus and the breaking of bread is key to the mystery of the Eucharist. Williams writes that "Jesus binds himself to vulnerability before he is bound (literally) by human violence. Thus, those who are at table with him, who include those who will betray, desert, and repudiate him, are, if you like, frustrated as betrayers, their job is done for them by their victim."[12]

> And so the sequence of transitions finally effects the transformation of the recipients of the bread and wine from betrayers to guests, whose future betrayals are already encompassed in the covenanted welcome enacted by Jesus. The eucharistic ritual narrative thus condenses into itself the longer and more diffuse historical sequence of passion and resurrection—the betrayal followed by divine vindication and return of Jesus as host at the table...What is thus laid out as a sequence, the discovery of the dependability of God's acceptance on the far side of the most decisive human rejection,

---

[9] *On Christian Theology*, 230.
[10] Rowan Williams, *Resurrection : Interpreting the Easter Gospel* (New York: The Pilgrim Press, 1984) 60.
[11] I Cor 11:23 RSV.
[12] *On Christian Theology*, 216.

is, in the action of the Last Supper, anticipated in a single gesture, the gesture in which Jesus identifies himself with the 'passive' stuff of the material creation.[13]

Williams goes on to say that this action "makes void and powerless the impending betrayal" and in fact, Jesus transforms his betrayers into "guests and debtors."[14] Because of what Jesus did (and does,) a covenant has been established "that cannot be negated by their unfaithfulness," and the result is that all future betrayers will be treated with the same generosity.[15] The "saving work of Christ comes to completion in renunciation, a surrender of control."[16]

In response to this, Williams once again emphasizes that constantly dying to self is the means of being faithful in the Church. Without this, the focus on self, the competitiveness, the selfishness, and the desire to dominate, soon overshadow the power and mystery of Christ's passion. It is only when one is engulfed in the loss of self that a truly joyous sense of the Resurrection can be embraced. At least for a moment each time the mystery of the Eucharist is celebrated, Christ's self-giving overwhelms selfishness and violence and betrayal of the participants and, as the American Prayer Book catechism states, there is a "foretaste of the heavenly banquet which is our nourishment in eternal life."[17]

It is the Eucharist that first brings and then keeps the community together in the awesome life, death and resurrection mystery. This mystery includes the "Great Cloud of Witnesses"[18] of martyrs from the days of the persecution of the primitive church to, and including, all the faithful departed today. Into this life, the curious and the casual, the powerful and the arrogant, the stranger and the abused, the wounded, the maimed, the retarded, the lame and mentally ill are brought together. The church gathered at the sacrament of the Eucharist is "oppressor and traitor...the penitent and the restored kin of Christ."[19] The Eucharist is both failure and hope, knowing that the assembled, transcending time and place, are "his betrayers, then as now."[20] Those gathered are with Christ at Gethsemane, in the upper room, and at the cross as well as the empty tomb.

The Eucharist is also a manifestation of creation.[21] Jesus is indeed the "Incarnate Word" through whom "all things were made."[22] At each celebration there is "the

---

[13] Ibid.

[14] Ibid.

[15] Ibid.

[16] Ibid., 217. "Sacramental practice seems to speak most clearly of loss, dependence and interdependence, solidarities we do not choose: none of them are themes that are particularly welcome or audible in the social world we currently inhabit as secular subjects." Ibid., 219.

[17] BCP, 860.

[18] Hebrews 12:1 RSV.

[19] *Resurrection*, 58.

[20] Ibid., 40.

[21] Ibid., 113.

[22] John 1:3 and the Nicene Creed.

embodiment of creation's hidden truth."[23] And from this hidden truth comes judgment and grace, words of comfort and the "call to transforming action."[24] Sacraments engage the church and the world by striving to make sense of the acts of God and the verities of the human condition, by implementing signs and symbols to convey deep truth that is impossible to explain or describe by the limitations of language.

Sacraments are also ways in which Christian communities try to make sense of the experience of holiness, that is the "otherness"of Christ.[25] Therefore sacraments are to be experienced in the "sacramental action..."[26] of the one who lived and died and lives again.[27] Jesus comes as the "other," the one who is manifested as both the intimate one and the one who is the stranger, the one who is known only in His self disclosure. For it is "the tension of 'otherness' [which] remains itself part of the fluid and dynamic nature" of both the celebration of the Eucharist and the mystery of Baptism.[28] These sacraments are the celebrations of God who is "committed to drawing our lives into the order of healing and communion." [29]

In closing, it must be noted that Williams sees the common experience of participation in baptism and the Eucharist as foundational for accommodating differences among Christians. Sacraments are celebrations of the risen Christ, who in dying to self, makes it possible for each Christian, in turn, to die to self, so that there indeed can be new life in Him. This new life, based in love and holiness, is the means of accommodating differences. This accommodation is only possible by an ongoing awareness that sacraments are means of covenant, and that by participating in them, the whole community of faith becomes an expression of the risen Christ.

---

[23]*Resurrection*, 114.

[24]Ibid., 114-115.

[25]"Sense" is used here both as a means of comprehending (understanding) and apprehending (to be caught up). It is the way in which the holiness of God can be discerned through the "senses." *On Christian Theology*, 201-202.

[26]Ibid., 206

[27]Williams does note, however, that it is perfectly appropriate to use consecrated objects of the Eucharist as the means of devotion, but this devotion must not supercede participation in the community's celebration and reception of the Eucharist itself. Ibid.

[28]Ibid., 207.

[29]Ibid.

CHAPTER VI

RESURRECTION AND THE COMMUNITY OF FAITH

Some critics of Williams' theology have expressed concern that he rejects the concept of a bodily resurrection. To clarify his position on this and other topics, he participated in an interview with *The Southern Cross,* a periodical of the Anglican Church of Australia. In it Williams affirms his belief in the bodily resurrection of Jesus. Here is his statement in part:

> I am completely committed to the bodily resurrection of Jesus—the empty tomb and the continuity of the pre- and post-resurrection body. Finding words for that, which everyone will immediately sign on to, is not easy. I have a slight hesitation myself about the expression 'physical resurrection', to the extent that it might suggest just the resuscitation of a corpse. It is physical in the sense that there's nothing left of Jesus in the tomb. All that was Jesus, Jesus is.[1]

Williams went on to admit in the article that some people thought his views to be a bit "wooly," but he just didn't know how to say it better. The intent of this chapter is to explore more fully his views on resurrection and how they are foundational for his understanding of the importance of common experience and accommodation of differences in establishing and maintaining unity in the church.

In an article about the resurrection he wrote for *The New Dictionary of Pastoral Studies,*[2] Williams begins by looking at "the two centuries immediately before the

---

[1]May 27, 2002

[2]Rowan Williams, "Resurrection," in *The New Dictionary of Pastoral Studies*, ed. Wesley Carr (London: SPCK, 2002), 315-316.

Christian era."[3] During this time of persecution, the concept of resurrection became intertwined with martyrdom; specifically of those faithful Jews, who were killed, would be the ones resurrected from the dead as vindication by God.[4] Williams notes that at that time resurrection conveyed a twofold purpose:

1. It vindicated those who suffered for their faithfulness
2. It humiliated and punished those who persecuted God's faithful people[5]

By the time of Jesus, some two centuries later, it was understood at least by the Pharisees that resurrection also included the ushering in of the New Age of the Messiah.[6] On the occurrence of the death and resurrection of Jesus, it soon became clear that it was in and from the community of faith that the presence of the risen Christ was most profoundly discerned. Said another way, it was in the "Body of Christ" that the resurrected Jesus had appeared and continues to appear to bring about reconciliation and new life to those who abandoned Him. Although sin and death, violence and vitriol, have not been eliminated, the presence of the resurrected Christ brings repentance, forgiveness, absolution and reconciliation, all critical components of unity. It is in this resurrection community that the stranger and the estranged are welcomed, acknowledging that all present are victims and victimizers, pain receivers and pain inflictors.

In his book *Resurrection: Interpreting the Easter Gospel,* Williams more fully develops his thoughts on the topic with observations about the resurrection accounts found in both the Gospels and the other writings of the New Testament. They seem somewhat disconnected, yet it is in this disconnectedness that something very strange and unusual happened. Stories of personal encounters with the Risen Christ were shared. Williams emphasizes that the stories of the resurrection are cohesive, what he calls a "family of beliefs (and) not a chaotic plurality."[7] They speak of a common experience. The narratives of the New Testament are stories of the witness of faithful people, both as eyewitnesses and, in turn, as witnesses to others. They all affirm the reality of the resurrection and together they form a community of faith, which bore witness to these stories, the "church in the New Testament period."[8] It was the great compulsion to share these stories about what God has done in Jesus that brought the wrath of the Sanhedrin down on these early disciples. But they would not be silenced. One of the first things they shared was the promise of the hope of absolution for those who killed Jesus.[9] Even in the face of persecution, it was announced that "Jesus who was deserted and executed is alive with God and also present" to any and all who would follow him.[10]

---

[3]Ibid., 315.

[4]Ibid., Williams refers to Daniel 12: 2 "And many of those who sleep in the dust of the earth shall awake, some to everlasting life and some to shame and everlasting contempt."

[5]Ibid.

[6]Ibid.

[7]Ibid., 2.

[8]Ibid., 3.

[9]Ibid., 2.

[10]Ibid., 1.

This is the Good News that was preached. From the first few chapters of the Acts of the Apostles, it is seen that the announcement of the death and rising of Jesus was not information given to an uninformed crowd. The hearers in Jerusalem were spectators or, perhaps, even participants in the events surrounding the triumphal entry into Jerusalem and the trial, crucifixion and resurrection of Jesus.[11] These people themselves are part of the story. The reality of the resurrection was proclaimed in the preaching of the disciples. It moved the stories from objective information to stories of common experience, shared in the community and accommodated as parts of the greater story.

It is this common experience of the resurrection which Williams sees as the grounds for unity in the church. He uses Jerusalem as a simile. Jerusalem is anyplace where the Church is "insistently and relentlessly...confronted...with a victim who is *our* victim."[12] Williams continues:

> When we make victims, when we embark on condemnation, exclusion, violence, the diminution or oppression of anyone, when we set ourselves up as judges, we are exposed to judgment (as Jesus himself asserts in Matt.7:1-2), and we turn away from salvation. To hear the good news of salvation, to be converted, to turn back, to the condemned and rejected, acknowledges that there is hope nowhere else.[13]

Whenever one recognizes "*one's victim as one's hope*"[14] then the resurrected Christ is present. He continues. Jerusalem exists where the only "pure victim, the one who unlike the rest of humanity is not *both* the oppressor and the victim"[15] is encountered and recognized. Jerusalem is where the sequence of crucifixion and resurrection are experienced today, in any form of violence and victimization.

When the risen Jesus is truly encountered and recognized, it is remembered that "when he was reviled, he did not revile in return; when he suffered, he did not threaten; but he trusted to him who judges justly."[16] The risen Christ is the one who suffered the crushing violence of the crucifixion. For Williams this exposes humanity's tendency to victimize with violence, a common experience. This is how he uses the simile of Jerusalem: it is anyplace where people, Christian or not, have experienced the crucified and risen Christ. They are themselves "guilty of the 'violence of the cross'" and they realize that their only hope and vindication is to "turn back to the victim,"[17] any victim. In so doing, they turn back to Christ. When is done consciously, for Williams, it is true conversion. For it is by turning to, and reconciling with, any-

---

[11]Ibid., 7
[12]Ibid., 11.
[13]Ibid. 11-12.
[14]Ibid.
[15]Ibid., 12.
[16]I Peter 2:23 RSV
[17]*Resurrection*, 26.

one who is one's victim, that one's eyes are opened to the risen Christ, who is the "pure victim, the carrier of mercy and acceptance."[18] Williams thinks that this should compel the believer to be sensitive to society's victims and to embrace a strong social conscience. But Williams does acknowledge that a sociological view of the resurrection does not exhaust his understanding. He indicates his orthodoxy by speaking of the "presence" of the risen Christ as the presence of God.[19] For Williams, it is a dialectic:

> The dialectic of the resurrection stories is the dialectic of all our worship and contemplation, so that to see in the risen Jesus both an endlessly receding horizon and a call to journey more and more deeply towards our centre and our home is to see him as God-like: more simply, to see him as *God* because he is the concrete form in which we encounter this infinity of challenge and infinity of acceptance most clearly and comprehensively.[20]

It is this encounter with the divine presence that allows, even causes the "memory of our responsibility for rejection and injury, for diminution of self and others" to come to the forefront of our consciousness.[21] To deny these memories is a great offense to God. But to remember them is to allow one to repent and accept absolution and be reconciled with God and others. This for Williams is a recovery of the past in hope. This is not regression, a return to the past; rather it is bringing the transformed past into the present with the hope and promise of redemption. "What happens in the resurrection is that this memory [of sin] is given back" to the risen Christ, "the victim who will not condemn" any who remember and repent.[22] Williams emphasizes that resurrection is not just for individuals; it is also expressed as a community event. Again, with the theme of repentance and absolution, he writes that whole communities need and do experience forgiveness and redemption. He notes that "forgiveness occurs not by a word of acquittal, but by a transformation of a world of persons."[23] Of all communities, it is the Church which must constantly seek forgiveness and reconciliation.

> The Church's work of judgment, its critical role in the world, is a nonsense (and worse) if criticism is not built into its own life and structures. Only a penitent Church can manifest forgiven-ness—a tautology, perhaps, but worth saying. A merely critical Church can reproduce in horrifying forms precisely those oppressive and exclusive relations which it exists to judge. It will pass sentence upon those beyond its boundaries, and so will be concerned about those boundaries and their exact definition.[24]

---

[18]Ibid.
[19]Ibid., 29.
[20]Ibid., 92.
[21]Ibid., 29.
[22]Ibid., 35.
[23]Ibid., 52.
[24]Ibid., 53.

The community of the risen Christ is gifted with the presence and power of the Holy Spirit, partly as a direct cause of the penitential observances of the church. As the church calls for and engages in true *metanoia* (the change of mind that is repentance), the risen Christ is there to forgive, embrace and embody the presence of God, both for the individual and the community as a whole. Note that it is a communal act. More than anything else, resurrection is relational. It is relationship with Christ, it is relationship with other Christians and it is relationship with the world. It is the ongoing relationship between members of the Body of Christ who have become part of Him through Baptism, and who now witness to the world. This makes Christ known uniquely and especially as a loving presence. In fact, resurrection may be likened "to the *embodied* love of God."[25] With this Williams sounds a warning to the church. He reminds the church that Christ is not only in midst of her, but He also "addresses the community from the *outside.*" Just as the church encounters the world, so Christ confronts the church from the world.[26] This is an ongoing reminder that the members of the church will continue to betray Christ, and that transcending time they seek to crucify Him over and over again. To confront this, Williams informs the reader that it is as a stranger that Christ came to his disciples on Easter morning.[27] The Risen Christ continues to come as a stranger to the church and to the world in the preaching of the Gospel, in the overall community of faith via the sacraments of baptism and Eucharist, in shared stories of the faithful and in the needs of the broken and estranged. Resurrection is the manifestation of the presence of Christ, and it is bedrock to Williams' beliefs.

In review, Williams affirms his belief in the bodily resurrection of Jesus, although it is more than just the "resuscitation of a corpse." For him, the bodily resurrection means that "there was nothing left of Jesus in the tomb." Resurrection is the manifestation of the full presence of Christ. His understanding of the resurrection comes from the witness of the New Testament church which shared a plethora, a family, of beliefs about the resurrection, which are all based in the common experience of the resurrection. This is a legacy that has been passed down to today. The gospel resurrection accounts speak not only to the objective reality of Jesus' resurrection, but also to the subjective experience of the risen Christ. This is both the heartfelt, individual encounter with the risen Jesus, and the sociological awareness that any victim, any where, is really a revictimization of Jesus. Williams reminds the church, that the risen Jesus came as a stranger to the disciples on Easter morning. And so, He comes to the church today in the forms of the broken, the alienated, the poor; as any victim. For Williams, it is in these social injustices that Christ own crucifixion is incarnated today. It is remedying these injustices that the resurrection, for Williams the embodied love of God, is affirmed and even relived. The final word, though, is that the death and resurrection is the triumph of love over violence and victimization. That is common experience and the means of accommodating differences.

---

[25]Ibid., 102.
[26]Ibid., 105.
[27]Ibid., 79.

CHAPTER VII

AUTHORITY IN THE CHURCH

For unity in the church to be effective, it must be under a mutually agreed upon authority, so that different perspectives can refer to a common source and thus be accommodated. Being under authority means accepting a "limiting of options" in life[1] In other words, authority gives *"definition."*[2] Whether it be the church, or any other community, authority exists to establish "a common order for the sake of the common good."[3] In essence, authority becomes a "political concept as soon as it is applied to the life of *any* community."[4] For Anglicans, the politics of the communion make the issue of authority complicated and often muddled. This is part of the Anglican ethos, and it is based in the term *Via Media.*

Via Media is central to the thought of Anglican luminaries from George Herbert to John Henry Newman.[5] It refers to the "middle road" between the Protestantism of Geneva and the Catholicity of Rome. This road is broad and the travelers are diverse. Although Rowan Williams does not make frequent use of this term in his writings, it is evident that his ecclesiology is grounded in this "middle road" of Anglicanism.

In conjunction with colleagues Geoffrey Rowell and Kenneth Stevenson, Williams has compiled an anthology of the writings of prominent Anglicans from the English Reformation through the end of the twentieth century. It is an examination of the thought of those whom Williams and his colleagues call the "*real* heirs" of clas-

---

[1]Rowan Williams, "Authority and the Bishop of the Church" in *Their Lord and Ours: Approaches to Authority, Community and the Unity of the Church,* ed. Mark Santer, (London: SPCK, 1982), 90.

[2]Ibid., 91.

[3]Ibid.

[4]Ibid., 92.

[5]F.L. Cross and E.A. Livingstone, ed., *The Oxford Dictionary of the Christian Church,* 3rd ed. (Oxford: Oxford University Press, 1970).

sical Anglicanism. It is a compilation of very diverse figures who all fit well under the name "Anglican."[6] They truly are examples of people who had a common experience of the Gospel, who interpreted that experience very differently, but were accommodated by the greater church.

Williams and his cohorts examine the three groups which are the primary expressions of this common experience of the Gospel in Anglicanism: Evangelicals, Catholics and Liberals. All have a place on the *via media*. Each claims to be rooted in the English Reformation. All agree upon the threefold authority of scripture, tradition and reason, but each has a different understanding of which is primary. For example, Evangelicals tend to look to scripture first and believe "that the English Reformation was an affirmation of the absolute supremacy of scripture all matters affecting the Church."[7] Evangelicals are inclined to believe that, in all generations, the Bible must be the basis for "purifying" the church from the taint of the world, the flesh and the devil.[8]

Catholics tend to look to the traditions of the church as their primary source of authority. Williams and his fellow authors write:

> Those from the catholic wing will stress the concern of sixteenth and seventeenth-century Anglicans to preserve the forms of ministry handed down from the earliest days of the Church, and their sense of spiritual and sacramental continuity with early Fathers and the faith of the 'undivided Church'; quite often *they* will add that the feverish intensity of the period distorted the proper character and calling of the Anglican Church by allying to various Protestant principles that were really extraneous to the central business of creating a reformed, non-papal Catholicism, based on a renewed sacramental life.[9]

Catholics tend to lean toward the idea that the purpose of the Reformation was to create an English catholic church which was free from Papal authority, but which continued in the authoritative tradition of the primitive church.

Liberals, tending to view reason as their chief authority, point to the early diversity of the great reformers and affirm that Anglicanism has not and should never identify with "specific theological principles, in contrast to the Reformed Churches of the continent of Europe."[10] Liberals, looking especially to Richard Hooker, are adamant that Anglicans have never been in the *sola scriptura* camp and therefore affirm that other sources of authority, specifically reason (in conjunction to a lesser degree with tradition) must constantly challenge the orthodoxy of the church. Too much emphasis on Biblical literalism makes them feel "that the essence of their Christian identity has been betrayed."[11]

---

[6]Geoffrey Rowell, Kenneth Stevenson and Rowan Williams, *Loves' Redeeming Work: the Anglican Quest for Holiness* (Oxford: Oxford University Press, 2001).
[7]Ibid., xxiii.
[8]Ibid.
[9]Ibid.
[10]Ibid.
[11]Ibid.

Accommodating the profound differences among these groups continues to be a daunting task. It is only possible by incorporating a language structure in both theology and liturgy that enables people from the various groups (and numerous subgroups in the Evangelical, Catholic and Liberal wings) to talk about and to God in ways that are not limited to those who "share their particular theological concerns."[12] The effect is that they value more the sharing of a common "Christian Life" and less the development or implementation of a "systematic theology."[13] For Williams, authority in the church is based largely on relationships and the consensus of the community. This is what was common among the central figures of the English Reformation; they were able to work and worship co-operatively because they did not emphasize a systematic source of authority, but instead they affirmed a "sense of what human life looks like when it is in the process of being transformed by God in Christ."[14] In other words, reflecting on God and His ways was intertwined with reflections on how humans "become holy," and a common experience of holiness is a foundational authority for Williams.[15] These early reformers, as much as they differed, all submitted to the authority of the common experience of holiness. They were united in affirming that holiness is more than subscribing to a set of doctrines. They differed in their emphases, but they recognized that "the job of theology [is] to draw out what might be, rather than to clear up all possible controversies before anyone is allowed to recognize holiness."[16] The great doctrinal themes of Grace, Atonement, Incarnation, Salvation, Resurrection and so forth are a "steady backdrop, sensed and believed,"[17] and this sensing and believing is a common experience which is authoritative and provides the means for accommodating some pretty diverse interpretations of the Gospel.

Williams looks to the primitive church to underscore his understanding of the authority of holiness. For example he lays a foundation for his belief that there was not a single interpretation of the faith for them, and consequently there was a certain creative tension among the variety of theological positions. Heresy came about only when there was too much emphasis on defining terms.

What the early Church condemned as heresy was commonly a tidy version of its language, in which the losses were adjudged too severe for comfort...The question would arise of whether the same God is still being spoken of; or whether a new version of the believing community's speech allowed as much to be said of the older version.[18]

---

[12]Ibid., xxiii-xxiv.
[13]Ibid., xxiv.
[14]Ibid.
[15]Ibid.
[16]Ibid., xxiv.
[17]Kenneth Leech and Rowan Williams, ed., "What is Catholic Orthodoxy?" *Essays Catholic and Radical* (London: Bowerdean Press, 1983), xxv.
[18]*On Christian Theology*, xii-xiii.

Williams maintains that authority in the church, then as now, rests on the community's experience of "Christian holiness, the unity anchored in the form of Christ."[19] In other words, holiness comes from Christ and, in fact, is Christ. This presence of Christ as the presence of holiness "has something to contribute to all human cultures, all human essays in the construction of meaning."[20]

This is where and how Christ's all encompassing holiness functions as a unifying source for the church. The holiness of Christ is an external force, surrounding the church with His presence and embracing the community in an act of unification. It is also an internal force within the church which draws people to Christ and to one another. Williams is aware that human free will can cause Christ's holiness to be deflected by the turmoil of unresolved theological issues (among other things.) But even here, the promise of holiness is unifying. Participation in conflict is, in some mystical way, participation in the crucifixion of Jesus. In the effort to be open to differences, Christians open themselves to the gift of Christ's suffering. Ironically, it is sin and the frailty of the human condition that leads the community to focus exclusively on dogma, instead of the actual presence of Christ. And this dogma, either the orthodox heritage and teaching of the Church or the liberal political correctness of the current age, can readily become rigid and authoritarian. Williams writes that dogma

> becomes empty and even destructive...when it is isolated from a lively and converting worship and a spirituality that is not afraid of silence and power-lessness. The more God becomes functional to the legitimizing either of the ecclesiastical order or private religiosities, the easier it is to talk of God, the less such talk gives place to the freedom of God. And that suggests that there is an aspect of dogmatic utterance that has to do with making it *harder* to talk to God.[21]

Williams believes that if dogma is too tightly defined, it is a stumbling block to holiness. It destroys community for the sake of correctness, and community, which is the true manifestation of the church's unity, takes precedence for Williams over theology. He believes that the essence of the church is community, and holiness is the authoritative glue that holds Christian community together. It "is a community enabled to live in provisionality without apathy or resignation...The Church is what, so to speak, promises the world to God, because the world's future is already represented by Christ."[22] The holiness of the church is manifested both as the "Spirit filled community" and the "sign of the Spirit" to the world.[23]

---

[19]Ibid., 26
[20]Ibid., 32
[21]Ibid., 84.
[22]Ibid., 101.
[23]Ibid., 124.

Although all members of the community are called to embrace and implement the holiness of Christ, it is the clergy who specifically are called upon by Williams to convey the "picture" of a holy assembly by the very act of presiding. Williams writes:

> If you want to know what the clergy are for, do not start with the pragmatic considerations, the jobs you would like clergy to do in running things or providing leadership...start with the *picture* of an assembly that in its formal structure and its disposition of responsibilities and its language, gesture and process draws you towards a contemplative understanding of the act of God in cross and resurrection and in the eternal love by which God is God.[24]

Among the clergy, it is the bishop that is most significant in Williams' thinking as a symbol and force of unity, for it is the bishop who is at the center of community life and authority. Williams asserts that the primary function of a bishop is to present the holiness of the gospel as the "means of incorporation into a worshiping – ritual sharing group," a group based on the "immersion and emergence" of baptism and the "regular and repeated nourishment" of the Eucharist.[25] This is the paschal mystery lived out in the community of faith and manifested in holiness. The purpose of a bishop is to present the gospel as the symbol and means of holiness, which is the embrace of a life giving, life affirming conveyance of grace.[26] As a means of practicality and expediency, the individuals who have this gospel message bestowed upon them, specifically priests, must then be "engaged most directly in enactment ... preaching, teaching, baptizing and celebrating the Eucharist.[27] This "brings the whole church into being and draws the multiple identities into a common one."[28] However, overseeing this is the bishop who facilitates a sense of the holiness "in the crucified and risen Christ."[29] As Williams points out, this must be done in concert with the whole of the community, not only gathered locally, but throughout the interconnectedness of the church. A bishop "cannot be a virtuoso soloist."[30] A bishop must always receive support from the ministries of his people, as well as extending his own ministry back to them. Succinctly, Williams states that the authority of a bishop is the "authority to unify." It is "not an authority to abolish or minimize conflict within the community."[31] Further, a bishop must refer all sides of a debate to the unifying holiness of the Good News of God in Christ.

In reflecting on Williams' view of authority, one can see the tension of striving to find a common theme in a communion which has three primary branches, the

---

[24]*Michael Ramsey*, 17.
[25]*Authority and Bishop*, 95.
[26]Ibid.
[27]Ibid., 96.
[28]Ibid., 97.
[29]Ibid., 98.
[30]Ibid., 99.
[31]Ibid.

Evangelical, the Catholic, and the Liberal, each looking to a different source of authority as being primary. Evangelicals look to scripture, Catholics tend to see the traditions of the church as primarily authoritative, and Liberals are inclined to view reason as preeminent. Williams offers another perspective. He believes that the shared stories of faithful people, an affirmation of a common experience of the Gospel, of coming together and discerning the holy in their midst, not just now but through the generations, acts as cohesion, and is thus ultimately authoritative. He believes that the effect of authority is more a sense of sharing a common life in Christ and less the development of systematic theology. Authority, for Williams, is based on solid relationships and community experiences of Grace. From this, a common experience of holiness can be made known which, for Williams, is the presence of Christ. All clergy, and especially bishops, are to bring together both the stories of faith and those who tell these stories in a cohesive fashion that does not eliminate conflict, but uses it as a means of conveying the mystery of the cross. This is the environment for holiness in the church and when lived out, it is the ultimate expression of Godly authority.

CHAPTER VIII

CRITICISM OF WILLIAMS' POSITIONS

Rowan Williams is not without critics. There are those on both the left and on the right, who disagree with him and do not find his positions unifying. For example, there are liberals who despair over his harsh criticism of abortion. Williams affirms that a fetus is a person from conception, and should be viewed and treated as such. He finds it ironic that when a mother is encouraged not to smoke or drink alcohol during her pregnancy, she is being advised to make healthy choices not only for herself, but for her unborn child as well.[1] However, when pictures of a twenty-four week old fetus were printed in a newspaper, the outrage of pro-choice forces was revealing, and rather disturbing. It acknowledges the "significance of sheer instinctive recognition of something human."[2] He observes that there are "different *levels* of dependence and biological organisation: at no point can we mark a transition from one kind of life to another."[3] He goes on to say that it is "more fashionable" to defend the moral rights of animals or even the environment than it is to try to "persuade people of the appropriateness of defending unborn humans."[4] It is ironic that in the name of "choice" a "moral issue" of such "decisive importance" is argued to destroy human life.[5] Pro-choice liberals despair over his position on abortion.

There are also political conservatives who disagree strongly with Williams. Cal Thomas, conservative Christian columnist, chides Williams for his equivocation about the September 11th, 2001 attack on the United States. Williams happened to be inside Trinity Church, Wall Street, making a presentation, just a few hundred yards from the World Trade Center, when it was attacked by Muslim terrorists. The church building

---

[1]Rowan Williams, *Lost Icons: Reflections on Cultural Bereavement* (Edinburgh: T&T Clark Ltd., 2000) 41.
[2]Ibid., 46.
[3]Ibid., 45.
[4]Ibid., 46.

and those inside, including Williams, escaped relatively unscathed. Instead of being critical of the attackers, Williams was more cautious. Almost a year later at "Greenbelt," a Christian arts festival at the Cheltenham racetrack in England, he was quoted by Thomas as saying that he (Williams) did not view the attack as "an act of war" and that the United States may actually have prompted the "savage attack." Again, Thomas quotes from Williams' speech. "The only thing I could feel grateful for on that day was of having some very slight sense of what it must be like to live under bombardment, under threat of death." Thomas makes this critique:

> This is classic theological and political liberalism. A murderer is not to be judged, but his victim should be condemned. If the murderer hadn't been provoked, he would have not killed. The murderer bears no true moral guilt for his action. The victim bears the burden in that he (or in this case the United States) goaded those poor souls to kill innocent passengers on the airplanes and thousands of others on the ground in New York and Washington D.C. The role of religious leaders in the aftermath of such a terrorist act, Dr. Williams says, is to engage in self-criticism and persuade the community to examine where it failed and what mistakes were made. "What we perhaps needed at a time of crisis like that is for people to be able to say there is something we have not understood, something we have not done," said Dr. Williams.[6]

The most consistent criticism of Williams, both from the left and from the right, is linked to what Geoffrey Rowell, Bishop of the Anglican Church in Europe, calls the "apophatic emphasis" of Williams' thought.[7] Humphrey Southern, an English cleric, offered this explanation in a paper entitled "The Impossibility of the Last Word: The Theology of Rowan Williams" that he presented at St. James Church in Sydney, Australia, on July 23, 2003. He critiques Williams' apophatic or *Via Negativia* perspective:

> Clearly the danger of *via negativia* is that taken to a logical extreme it leaves its followers unable to say anything about anything (or at least of importance, which is the theological task). Indeed, in the Eastern Orthodox Church (where it is greatly stressed) the *via negativia* is known as the "apophatic" tradition, where *apophosis* may be taken to be the opposite of *emphasis*: reticence, rather than definitiveness in pronouncement. Wordless silence in the face of the almightiness of God is, of course, a wholly appropriate reaction, but for useful productive theological activity to continue, it is necessary

---

[5]Ibid.

[6]Cal Thomas, "The Great Welch Disappointment" *Townhall.com,* September 2, 2002 (downloaded May 31, 2004). Available from http://www.townhall.com/columnists /calthomas/printct20020902.shtml.

[7]Geoffrey Rowell, "Resourced by the Grace of Christ," *The Church Times* (2 April, 2004).

for the *via negativia* to be tempered by some conter-vailing encouragement to communicate...it is worth remembering that the apophatic method which has had a powerful influence on Williams, begins in silence.[8]

Ironically, Williams' reluctance to take rigid stands may in fact be a key component in keeping the Anglican Communion together. If reticence is his primary means of conveying his positions, it does leave room for disagreement among church members, and disagreement voiced, according to Williams, is a means of accommodating differences and maintaining unity, because it is an expression of the right of each member to express belief and not be ostracized. He does not want to shut down discussions prematurely. In his book *Lost Icons,* Williams confirms his rationale for his reticence.

> Those who claim to speak in the name of God will always be dangerously (exhilaratingly) close to the claim that in their speech, their active presence, the absent God who is never an existent among others is actually present: a claim of stupendous importance in legitimating any bid for power. Here, it says, is a concrete presence that will tell you what you are. The religious ideologue may say—or seem to be saying—that it is in *his* 'other' that you will find your identity (and I do mean 'his' given the history of religious hierarchy in most human cultures); and this will effect a definitive closure on what you are entitled to say about yourself. You are required or desired to satisfy the demands mediated by religious law; that is what you are for, all you are for.[9]

To counter those who are too certain about Christ, Williams offers uncomfortable metaphors. Here are three examples. The first is Christ as the "riddler." "Christ's is the kingship of a riddler, the one who makes us strangers to what we think we know."[10] Williams insists that when a Christian is too certain, Christ confronts with uncertainty and even confusion which leads to "repentance without which there is no truth."[11] A second image which he points to is the helpless Christ child as the one who is unable to speak clearly and yet screams as any baby, and "we are confronted by something strange and uncomfortable...he confronts us with the alarming, mysterious, shattering strangeness of God."[12] A third image is that of God "as a spastic child who can communicate nothing but his presence and inarticulate wanting."[13]

---

[8]Humphrey Southern, "The Impossibility of the Last Word: The Theology of Rowan Williams," Anglicans Together (downloaded June 7, 2004). Available from http://www.anglicanstogether.org3.html.

[9]*Lost Icons*, 162.

[10]Rowan Williams, Ray *of Darkness* (Cambridge, Massachusetts: Cowley Publications, 1995), 110.

[11]Ibid., 111.

[12]Ibid., 28.

[13]Ibid., 123.

Williams likens this to the great inarticulate suffering of Christ on the Cross. There is no room for articulate theological speculation. Only in unarticulated groaning can the common experience of alienation and frustration and fear and helplessness, common to all people, be conveyed.

Coming at the issue of helplessness from the human perspective, Williams refers to St. John of the Cross and the "night of the spirit" (or "night of the soul") which he argues is the "only defense religion ever has or ever will have against the charge of a cosy fantasy."[14] He refers to it as

> a wall in the way...it is the evacuation of meaning. We have been going round and round the paths, and suddenly we see that our path goes round a hole, a bottomless pit. In the middle of all our religious constructs—if we have the honesty to look at it—is an emptiness. It makes nonsense of all religion, conservative or radical and all its piety.[15]

Williams draws insights (as mentioned in a previous chapter) from St. John, a sixteenth century Carmelite monk whose torment, estrangement from his order, imprisonment and resultant anguish led to an experience of intimacy with God. Williams writes that "Intimacy with God means refusing all consoling substitutes for God and bearing the consequences."[16] Williams is blunt:

> You must recognise that God is so unlike whatever can be thought or pictured, that, when, you have got beyond the stage of self-indulgent religiosity there will be nothing you can securely know or feel. You face a blank; and any attempt to avoid that or shy away from it is a return to playing comfortable religious games. The dark night is God's attack on religion."[17]

This perspective is criticized because it comes very close to saying that there is no power in the presence of Christ for those who call upon him for help, a concept that is contrary to much of the New Testament. For instance, Jesus states in Mark 11: 24, "whatever you ask in prayer, believe that you have received it., and it will be yours."[18] In Luke 11: 9-13 Jesus says,

> Ask, and it will be given to you; seek, and you shall find; knock and the door will be opened to you. For everyone who asks, receives, and he who seeks finds, and to him who knocks it will be opened. What father among you, if his son asks for a fish, will instead of a fish give him a serpent; or if he asks for an egg, will give him a scorpion? If you then, who are evil, know

---

[14]Ibid., 80.
[15]Ibid., 81.
[16]Ibid., 83.
[17]Ibid., 82.
[18]RSV

how to give good gifts to your children, how much more will the heavenly Father give the Holy Spirit to those who ask him?[19]

Or again, in John 14:13-14 Jesus speaks to his disciples and by implication to all Christians: "Whatever you ask in my name, I will do it, the Father may be glorified in the Son: if you ask anything in my name, I will do it."[20]

This leads to another area of controversy. For Williams, the historical Jesus does not "exhaust the divine," but instead is but one of several means by which people may be unified to God, but still may be estranged from one another. He asserts that

> we know that the historical form of Jesus, in which we see creation turning on its pivot, *does not exhaust the divine.*[ed.] We know that the unification of all things through Christ is not a matter of a single explanatory scheme being manifested to us, but of the variousness of human lives being drawn into creative and saving relationship to the divine and not to each other."[21]

What must happen to all who would seek God, no matter what the tradition, is that they eventually "go into the desert when the security of pictures and ideas fades away, where all theologies finally give way to God."[22] Williams states that in this encounter

> all we meet is the silence, a kind of annihilating judgment on all we say. Christ can bear all sorts of interpretations, and we can't expect him to tell us which he likes. We can draw little balloons coming out of his mouth as much as we like. What does that tell us? The vulgarity of the analogy under-lines the futility of the exercise. [23]

It is in this context that Williams becomes most critical of an interpretation of scrip-ture which is holistic and authoritative. For example, he says that some fragile people need to be protected *from* some passages of scripture because they (these weak people) are ill-prepared to deal with the "strangeness and sometimes the terror of the Word of God to fragile minds."[24] He goes on: "We read with a sense of our own benighted savagery in receiving God's gift, and our solidarity with those writers of scripture caught up in the blazing fire of God's gift who yet struggle with it, misapprehend it and misread it."[25] He is most critical of the *Revelation of St. John at Patmos.* Will-iams believes that the book contains two scripts, one which has a "haunting authority"

---

[19]RSV

[20]RSV

[21]*On Christian Theology*, 178. Italics by author.

[22]*Ray of Darkness*, 92.

[23]Ibid.

[24]*Ray of Darkness*, 98.

[25]Ibid., 136.

while the other is "tightly written, pen driving into cheap paper, page after page of paranoid fantasy and malice, like the letters clergymen frequently get from the wretched and disturbed."[26] He does concede that even the disturbing parts contribute to the hearing of the Word of God, but it is possible only in stark contrast with the authoritative parts:

> Perhaps, as we read the Revelation of John, we should let its ugly and diseased elements speak to us in this way. The very disorder, madness and vengefulness of certain passages can help us to hear more clearly the depth and authority of others...The rantings of John the Divine about his theological rivals are the by-product of the very vision of the Living One that shows these ravings for what they are, by showing the radical and unconfined purpose of God in Jesus Christ.[27]

Williams' criticism is not limited to St. John of Patmos. He believes that none of the biblical writers were infallible in their reception, nor in their conveyance of the material. He reacts to what he views as creeping fundamentalism in the church.

> "For the fundamentalist, the will of God is clearly ascertainable for all situations, either through the plain words of scripture (as received in a particular, but unacknowledged convention of reading) or with the aid of supernatural direct prompting. Christian revelation is there to offer clear and important information – how to be right."[28]

It seems that Williams paints with a broad brush in his criticism of scripture, as indicated above. Many conservative evangelicals, who are not fundamentalists, who accept the basic tenets of the higher critical method, still acknowledge that any call to trump any portion of the Biblical text with external sources must be viewed with a jaundiced eye. They are uncomfortable with Williams' kind of biblical interpretation. It is argued that Anglicans have never been in the *sola scriptura* camp of many in the protestant traditions. But Anglicans do have the statement from the Chicago/Lambeth Quadrilateral referring to the Holy Scriptures of the Old and New Testaments as "'containing all things necessary to salvation' and as being the rule and ultimate standard of faith."[29] Although Williams does not refute this, it is clear from his writings that he views the cohesiveness of scripture with some skepticism. He writes:

> In the old [sic] and New Testaments alike, unity is evidently articulated through *analogy*; divine events, persons, patterns of behaviour are recon-

---

[26]Ibid., 94.
[27]Ibid., 97-98.
[28]Ibid., 193.
[29]BCP, 877.

structed in writing and in the editing process of canonical formation so as to manifest a shared form, a family resemblance. This works in a particularly interesting way when Christian writers claim for their own the heroes of Jewish scriptures, so that these figures become resources for the self-understanding of the ordinary Christian convert. [30]

Another area of criticism concerns Williams' view of sin and salvation. For Williams, sin is not so much breaking the laws of God as it is falling prey to the forces of the world, the flesh and the devil which corrupt people and lead them away from God. Jesus knows what is in us.[31] He knows that when Christians sin against one another, they victimize each other. For Williams, to sin is to victimize, whether it be against another person or God through Jesus on the cross. "God is the ultimate victim of all human cruelty, says the gospel: God bleeds for every human wound. Inasmuch as we do good or ill to any human person, it is done to God."[32] This leads to Williams' understanding of the doctrine of atonement. It is one of empathy. In every extremity, every horror and pain, Jesus is accessible as the one who continues to make God's loving presence wholly present in the depth of his own anguish and abandonment.[33] The wonder of the cross is that it provides hope for both the victimizer and the victim. Jesus atones human victimizing by bearing hatred and violence; he empathizes with the victim by Himself being a victim and gives hope by transcending the victimization into the hope of the resurrection. Williams states:

> "If there is a God whose will is for the healing of men and women, he can heal only by acting in the worldliness of the world, in and through the vortex of loss and death. He must share in condition of our sickness, our damnation, so as to bring his life and his fullness into it.[34]

Although Williams makes thoughtful points, one wonders, "How far does this go?" Is salvation universal? Is it only for victims and repentant victimizers and no one else? Is it for adherents of other religious beliefs? Is there divine and eternal penalty for unrepentant sin? Gary J. Williams, conservative evangelical Anglican, observes that Archbishop Williams offers a doctrine that is troublesome for many evangelical Anglicans. "The doctrine that Jesus bore in our place the judicial wrath of God which sin deserved has been displaced by the idea that he became the victim of human hatred."[35] The seemingly active refutation of penal judgment by a righteous God is troubling. Further Archbishop Williams' sense of salvation seems to be

---

[30]*On Christian Theology* , 22-23.

[31]*Ray of Darkness*, 11.

[32]Ibid., 51.

[33]Ibid., 30.

[34]Ibid., 189.

[35]G.J. Williams, *The Theology of Rowan Williams: An Outline, Critique and Consideration of It's Consequences*, Latimer Studies, 28.

more sociological and psychological (victim and victimizers) than it does judicial. It suggests a therapeutic view of salvation which is only fulfilled in a just community (the church). As Gary J. Williams states, it "suggests a worrying lack of familiarity with what so many of the people he will be leading believe."[36]

Perhaps the most controversial of all Williams' ethical positions is his decision to support committed homosexual partnerships. He pointedly criticizes orthodox, conservative evangelicals and Catholics, who strongly disapprove of homosexual relations as being caught up in "panic stricken moralism."[37] He goes on to say, "I really do suspect that some of the frenzied anxiety about homosexuality arises less from moral disapproval than from the resentful sense that the homosexual is a kind of mocking *parody* of what most people assume sexual desire to be about."[38] Williams acknowledges that he has knowingly ordained at least one man who was in a committed homosexual relationship because he trusted that the man had a call to the priesthood and that he would not be a scandal to the church.[39] Williams' criteria for all those seeking ordination, whether straight or gay, is that they will do the things that build up the Body of Christ.

Williams is not just a proponent of gay and lesbian stable, long term relationships. He is also interested in reevaluating all sexual activity. In his 1989 lecture, "The Body's Grace," Williams sets forth a case for reconsidering sexual ethics. He maintains that the Christian community's task is to order "our relations [so] that human beings may see themselves as *desired.*"[40] This is the link to sex. In any authentic sexual encounter, the body is the manifestation of desire, both for giving and receiving. For Williams, this mutual desire is an expression and experience of grace, hence the title,"The Body's Grace." Williams defines an "authentic" encounter as one in which the "other" is viewed not as an "object," but as the one in which the self has been abandoned into appropriate desire. Williams writes that "in sexual relations I am no longer in charge of what I am."[41] Each person must be motivated by appropriate desire whether it is gay or straight. Appropriate desire must be an act of total self giving. Selfishness alone, therefore distorts any and all sexual encounters. For Williams, selfishness is more the issue than sexual orientation. Any non-self abandoning sex is not good. This is why rape, incest, pedophilia, and so forth are wrong. In these instances the other is used and the focus is on self gratification, not true mutual desire. There is something uneven about these behaviors. They are distorted and "distorted sexuality is the effort to bring my happiness back under my control and to refuse to let my body be another person's perception."[42]

---

[36]Ibid., 29.
[37]*Lost Icons*, 171.
[38]Ibid., 172-173.
[39]*Canterbury Tale.*
[40]Rowan Williams, "The Body's Grace" (London: Lesbian and Gay Christian Movement and the Institute for the Study of Christianity and Sexuality, 2nd ed., 2002) 3.
[41]Ibid., 4.
[42]Ibid., 5.

Williams sees committed, long term homosexual relationships as perfectly acceptable as long as each person views the sexual encounter as self giving rather than self serving. British journalist Graham Turner writes:

> Since physical sex is not always tied to procreation, he [Williams] believes that there is a good case not merely for recognizing same-sex relationships but also for at least considering the possibility that they may be legitimate in God's eyes—always providing that they are stable and faithful...He would not want to call them marriages.[43]

However, Williams even challenges the common understanding that heterosexual marriage is the only appropriate way and means of expressing sexual love. In fact, he believes that these officially "sanctioned" heterosexual relationships are all too often destructive. He writes, "the facts of the situation are that an enormous number of 'sanctioned' unions are a framework for violence and destructiveness on a disturbing scale."[44] Williams also desires to contradict any rejection of homosexual practice on the basis of its unreproductive nature.[45] He points out that in the New Testament neither Jesus nor Paul argue for the ability to reproduce as a basis for heterosexual marriage. In fact, Williams argues that there is no reason to reject same sex relationships as being sinful unless one uses "an abstract fundamentalist deployment of a number of very ambiguous texts." Conservative evangelicals bristle at this.

Gary J. Williams writes that

> The core of the conservative argument and the premise on which those texts themselves are built is the biblical doctrine of creation. This is not an isolated text, it is a reading of Genesis 1-2 in the light of the key role in the canon as a whole and especially in the teaching of Jesus, where it has a normative function in sexual ethics (e.g. Matthew 19:3-12). For Jesus, the account of creation serves as the paradigm which God has set out for his world and relations within it. That is the basis for rejecting same-sex relations which does not appeal to reproductivity, and which is based on neither fundamentalism nor non-scriptural theory.[46]

In a sermon entitled "Is there a Christian Sexual Ethic" from his book *Ray of Darkness,* Williams lays out his understanding of an appropriate sexual ethic:

> Our sexual lives are about making sense of the oddities and uncontrollabilities, tragedies and farces, of bodily existence; a Christian sexual ethic ought to be saying before all else that there is a distinctively

---

[43]*Canterbury Tale.*
[44]"The Body's Grace," 7.
[45]Ibid., 10.
[46]Gary Williams, 35

Christian sense to be made, the sense God makes in the life, death, and resurrection of Jesus where flesh itself carries the meaning of God's Word.[47]

There is biblical precedent to view God's relationship with His people as akin to the relationship between a husband and wife.[48] But Archbishop Williams doesn't stop there. Again, Gary J. Williams offers this critique:

> Williams goes beyond identifying even heterosexual marriage with the desire of God for his people, which is the only identification we find in Scripture. He jumps straight to arguing that homosexual activity which entails the genuine communication of sexual desire is legitimate. There are thus two leaps here. One is from the desire of love of God for his people to human *sexual* desire, and the other is from heterosexual biblical examples to homosexual acts."[49]

A central precept for Rowan Williams is the need for loss of self if one is to be truly faithful. The loss of self is foundational for gracious sex. He believes that all faithful, monogamous, sexual relationships can be holy if there is indeed a loss of self simultaneously with the sense of being desired by the beloved. Any and all sexual activity must not be selfish if it is to be holy.

However, enough furor has been raised about his views on human sexuality that prior to his enthronement as Archbishop of Canterbury, Williams wrote an open letter to his fellow Primates of the Anglican Communion concerning this issue on July 23, 2002. His aim was to calm the storm about his views on human sexuality. He asserts:

> that an archbishop is not someone elected to fulfil a programme or manifesto of his own devising, but to serve the whole Communion. He does not have the freedom to prescribe belief for the Church at large...my ideas have no authority beyond that of an individual theologian. Second, the Lambeth resolution of 1998 declares clearly what is the mind of the overwhelming majority in the Communion, and what the Communion will and will not approve or authorise. I accept that any individual diocese or even province that officially overturns or repudiates this resolution poses a substantial problem for the sacramental unity of the Communion.[50]

Williams seems to be a man of his word. After the Episcopal Church in the United States endorsed the consecration of V. Gene Robinson, an openly gay man living in a same sex relationship, to become bishop of New Hampshire and the diocese of New

---

[47]*Ray of Darkness*, 144.
[48]For example see the Book of Hosea and Jeremiah 31:32.
[49]G. J. Williams, 34.
[50]*The Mandate,* September/October 2002 vol.21 Number 5, 16.

Westminster, Canada decided to provide official blessings of same sex relationships, Williams has gone on record to distance himself from these decisions.[51] As late as October of 2003, Williams wrote that in spite of his training as a theologian and teacher which led him to his liberal views on human sexuality and other areas, he affirms the over-riding position of Anglican bishops throughout the world. He has a new role as Archbishop of Canterbury which brings with it obligations to maintain unity based on the authority of "the Bible and basic Christian belief."

> I'm a theologian by training and I've been a teacher of theology for a lot of my ministry and teachers of theology tend to have views on all sorts of things and they have to engage with colleagues and students with very varied opinions. But no pastor or bishop holds a post in which their task is to fight for the victory of their personal judgments as if those were final or infallible. My first task is that of any ordained teacher which is to point to the source without which none of our activity would make sense—the gift of God as it is set before us in the Bible and Christian belief.[52]

In review, it must be accentuated that Rowan Williams has many critics. Some on the left are concerned about his support of abortion. Some political conservatives criticize his views, especially in light of the September 11th attack on United States. Critics of his theology are frustrated by his apophatic tendency to be fuzzy and unclear. However most criticism comes from the orthodox in the church. There are conservative Catholic and Evangelical Anglicans who are frustrated by his liberal views of scripture, his argument that sin is more about victimizing others than it is about breaking God's holy laws, and his views of salvation which seem to be more psychological and sociological than theological. His most controversial views regard human sexuality. As Archbishop of Canterbury, he promises to soft pedal his views on human sexuality, in deference to the opposition he has received throughout the communion.

Ironically, his apophatic tendencies, frustrating as they are to some, and demonstrated by his reluctance to be emphatic in his pronouncements, make it is easier for divergent factions in the communion to share common experiences and accommodate differences, and therefore to maintain the unity of the church.

---

[51]See "A Statement by the Primates of the Anglican Communion meeting in Lambeth Palace" Oct.16, 2003.

[52]BBC News/UK July 23, 2002 Downloaded September 3, 2002.

CHAPTER IX

COMMON EXPERIENCE AND THE ACCOMMODATION OF DIFFERENCES: THE BASES FOR UNITY

Rowan Williams is concerned about maintaining unity in the Anglican Communion. In an interview with Roy Hattersley of the *Guardian* dated July 11, 2004, Williams emphasizes the importance of accommodation in maintaining unity in the church. In reference to the current conflict about homosexuality which threatens to fracture the Anglican Communion, Williams stresses that maintaining unity is a basic principle of "being" the church. In an era of mistrust and suspicion, finding ways to communicate, of even wanting to communicate, is paramount if the Anglican Communion is to stay together. He specifically refers to the 1998 Lambeth Resolution which stated clearly that homosexual behavior was incompatible with scripture and the historic teachings of the church. He was troubled by that decision, but believes that he must support it as Archbishop of Canterbury. He states that

> unity is a principle...it is all to do with a calculation that goes something like this. The decision was one which severely ruptured a whole set of relationships which are not about structural harmony but about mutual learning and mutual giving— relationships, let's say between churches in the developing world and the Church here or the Church in the States. To rupture these relationship would be bad for the Church, not as an institution, but as a community... making people feel they have not been taken seriously....[1]

---

[1] Roy Hattersley, "Just Williams" *Guardian*, July 11, 2004. Available from www.guardian.co.uk/print/0,3858,4968374-103602,00.html

Williams goes on:

> I have had it borne on me—I do not mean by weighty figures but borne in
> by the office—that, as Archbishop, I have to keep as many voices in play as
> possible...The voices in the developing world, people who regularly feel
> marginal in pretty well every respect, this is another turn of the screw for
> them. I'm serious about the international dimension here. That is probably
> what weighs with me most, personally and emotionally.[2]

However, when he hears what he considers to be "deeply prejudiced voices coming
out of the church" against homosexuals, he reminds them that part of this same
Lambeth Resolution was the promise to listen to the voices of gays and lesbians.
"We have that commitment as well." [3]

The tension among all sides seems to be growing. In the current climate of the
church, common experience of the gospel, in the form of heart felt encounters with
Christ, common participation in the sacraments, mutual affirmation of the creeds and
other basic tenets of the catholic faith, and an affirmation of the authority of holiness,
are being trumped by significant differences. In his book *Lost Icons: Reflections on
Cultural Bereavement,* Williams lays out five things which make accommodation
possible. They are charity, shame, honor, remorse and comedy. The foundation for all
accommodation is charity. In contrast, he sees competitiveness as the antithesis of
charity, for competitiveness is structured for winning and losing, and it seems that
the competing factions in the church have become competitive in their confronta-
tions with those with whom they differ. Charity transcends winning and losing. So,
especially in the church, charity, that is, mutually affirming, loving interaction which
is cooperative rather than competitive, thwarts resentment and mistrust. This is not
easy. People are self-centered. They put personal wants and needs ahead of those of
others and charity becomes de-emphasized. For Williams, the key to charitable behavior, both in and out of the Church, is to engage in conversation about areas of
difference. He writes that charitable interaction

> doesn't get done without a recognition that my good or dignity has no sub-
> stance, no life, without someone else's good or dignity being involved...the
> ideal position is one in which an indefinite number of agents perceive their
> welfare as including their relations to each other and their consent to an
> enjoyment of each others flourishing.[4]

Realistically, Williams acknowledges that there is a "spectrum of different types of
encounters" which range from casual discussion to dealing with mutual crises. But

---

[2]Ibid.
[3]Ibid.
[4]Rowan Williams, *Lost Icons: Reflections on Cultural Bereavement* (Edinburgh: T&T Clark
LTD, 2000) 77.

when conversations are shared, charitable relationships are both formed and strengthened.[5] But it is not easy. As Williams notes, "there is no simple path to charity." [6] One can look to scripture and find a good outline for charitable interaction. Using the *Authorized* or *King James* version of scripture, it states:

Charity suffereth long, and is kind; charity envieth not; charity vaunteth not itself; is not puffed up, Doth not behave itself unseemly, seeketh not her own, is not easily provoked, thinketh no evil; Rejoiceth not in iniquity, but rejoiceth in the truth; Beareth all things, believeth all things, hopeth all things, endureth all things. Charity never faileth....[7]

This is the very stuff of God and Williams affirms that it is available to all as a common experience and it is critical in accommodating differences. As the Apostle Paul states, we *see through a glass darkly..."* [8] Williams would say that no Christian has full clarity of vision. Therefore, the attitude of charity is needed to accommodate one another, trusting that the experiences of Christ, in a plethora of forms, will be affirmed, not as chaos, but as that which is not yet clear, yet common. Until Christians can meet fully *face to face* [9] in Christ, then there must be trust that Christ does reveal Himself in a myriad of ways and yet as truly common experience. This is Christian charity at work in the Body. The key is to keep alive the conversation about the experiences of the presence of Christ.

For conversation to continue, a sense of honoring all participants is needed to accommodate differences in the Church. He writes that "honour formalizes systems of *recognition,* grounds upon which conversation can proceed..."[10] Honor affirms the worth of all participants in the conversation, specifically those on the opposite side of the conflict. If honor is to be implemented, it requires conversation and affirmation.[11] This is basic to the gospel message. Jesus is clear in Matthew 5:43-44a,

You have heard it was said, 'You shall love your neighbor and hate your enemy.'
But I say to you, Love your enemies and pray for those who persecute you...[12]

For Williams, it is this recognition of the basic worth of those in opposition that is the grounding for affirmation of mutual honor. When the opponent is loved and honored, meaningful dialogue can take place.

Ironically, for Williams, shame and remorse are necessary for honor and charity

---

[5]Ibid., 82.
[6]Ibid., 85.
[7]I Corinthians 13: 4-8a.
[8]Ibid., verse12.
[9]Ibid.
[10]*Lost Icons*, 99.
[11]Ibid., 113.
[12]RSV.

to be manifested in the exchange of differences. Shame is based on remorse, which Williams states is"finding the self in others."[13] He writes:

> *shame* is both a personal and a social penalty...[It is] a real restriction on what I am able to think and feel about myself, as much as on what others think of me, make of me, say to me and understand about me.[14]

Shame is linked with empathy and true compassion, which connects people without oppression. Shame becomes destructive when people don't talk to each other during times of conflict. Honor counters shame by affirming the worth both of self, and of those on the other side of the conflict. However, without the feeling of shame and remorse, honor is often absent, because it slides into a self-righteousness, which is not grounded in charity. Remorse is needed if the full impact of a charitable encounter is to occur. Remorse is finding the self in others and hence it is "not melancholy but regret."[15] True remorse, which is akin to shame, is actually a celebration of "the vulnerable and even the comic."[16] What makes these encounters between conflicting parties "comic rather than tragic is that the characters *survive"* [17] Comedy "enacts a kind of conviction that finally delivers human welfare or reconciliation in some process supremely indifferent to the images human beings construct of themselves."[18] When accommodation, based on a desire to maintain or even establish charitable, honorable community, supercedes a strongly held position on say, sexuality, then comedy becomes a buffering source of grace. Williams even suggests that burlesque or satire point to the absurdity of stringent positions that do not accommodate differences.

> By burlesque, I mean simply evocations of the unexpected or embarrassing, episodes of broadly sketched absurdity: banana skins. And by satire, I mean the pointed localised depiction of abuses and self-deceptions, designed to shame or ridicule groups, to diminish their public 'honour', with the longer aim of making some sorts of untruthful, self-regarding behaviour more risky and unattractive.[19]

Comedy is a celebration of life and joy and hope in the midst of chaos and confusion. When chaos and confusion are not allowed to dominate, there is always hope for accommodation and even reconciliation, fostered not only with the comedy, by charity, honor, shame and remorse as well. When these five elements are present accommodation and the hope of unity are always possible.

---

[13]Ibid., 111.
[14]Ibid., 99.
[15]Ibid., 116.
[16]Ibid., 131.
[17]Ibid., 131-132.
[18]Ibid., 132.
[19]Ibid., 133.

CHAPTER X

CONCLUSION

As Archbishop of Canterbury, Rowan Williams has the ability to seek, to see and to bear witness to the presence of the risen Christ in the most unusual and difficult circumstances. He is a catholic in the broad, universal sense of the word, always striving to find ways of including folks while affirming the basics of the faith. He celebrates the "the one Christ [who] appears in the real diversity of many lives."[1] His understanding of unity in the church is based on common experience and the accommodation of differences.

He is a complex man who espouses complex views which are subtle to the point of being apophatic. He errs on the side of inclusivity. He strives to keep open theological options until they have been freely and fairly resolved. For example his seminal work on what he sees as the orthodoxy of Arius, generally considered to be a heretic, is in itself a statement of inclusivity, a key component of unity. He also links historical characters of the church, people who differed greatly in their understanding of being Christian, yet, Williams claims, they were unified in a common experience of the Risen Christ. They found ways to accommodate their differences, to establish and maintain unity in the Church.

For Williams, the community is the primary expression of the Risen Christ and that is the reason for his commitment to unity. However, because of the pressures of the world and sin, there must be an undergirding desire for holiness of life, both for individuals and for the community as a whole, to be both faithful and unified. He affirms all things "that make it possible to live a holy life and the criteria by which Christians recognize this or that life as holy."[2] When inevitable conflicts come and

---

[1]*Living Tradition*, 41.

[2]Rowan Williams, "The Seal of Orthodoxy": Mary and the Heart of Christian Doctrine," *Say Yes to God: Mary and the Revealing of the Word Made Flesh* ed. Martin Warner (London: Tufton Books, 1999), 15.

bring tension, he believes that they can be the means of life-giving, grace-filled tension, if the various factions will take time to talk and pray and reflect together. For example, if division exists in the church among liberal, catholic and evangelical branches, it can be overcome only by finding common vocabulary that describes common experiences. This language (found specifically for Anglicans in the various forms of the *Book of Common Prayer,*) provides the means for agreed upon prayer and a liturgical framework of sacraments. Coming together is an act of trusting Him who was killed, but who overcame death and the grave. This is unity in Jesus that can be found nowhere else and Christians of every ilk are to stand firm with and in Him. Key to this is Williams' constant call to "die to self" so that Christ will be made known in the life of the individual, the community and out in the world.

In his enthronement sermon, Williams stated: "we learn painfully and quickly that we cannot hold our own [in the church] by our own strength; it is Jesus's gift in life and death and resurrection that makes it possible for us to stand with him, breathing his breath, his Spirit."[3] In order to communicate this, the Church must use language carefully. The words of the community must be based on "the Bible and its shared life of prayer," because the "Church can't believe and say whatever it likes, for the very sound reason that it is a community of people who have been changed because and only because of Jesus Christ."[4]

Williams affirms the importance of the work of God the Holy Spirit. If it were not for the ongoing support of the Holy Spirit, which he refers to as "that absolute Truth, the unfolding light which is God,"[5] there would be no church. Williams maintains that when competing factions in the church believe that they stand alone with Christ, all conversation becomes mere theory and nothing changes or grows. He maintains that five things are needed to accommodate differences in the church: charity, shame, honor, remorse and comedy. Underlying this, however, is the understanding that the full revelation of Christ has not occurred. Until then, he affirms that there is a common experience of the Lord, but it is expressed as a family of beliefs, and not as a tight, closely defined statement. He makes this observation. "On the day of Judgment, says Jesus, looking back at the towns where he ministered, the people who are in trouble are those who have seen everything and grasped nothing; who know about everything about bread except that you are meant to eat it."[6] If the church is to be cohesive, it is to share bread, literally and metaphorically. The Risen Christ is encountered and consumed in the broken and shared bread of the Eucharist, and in the broken and shared lives of those who are part of the Body. When this happens there is a common experience of grace; there is truly an accommodation of differences and from this comes a true sense of unity. Sharing bread is the metaphor for reaching out to the world in love and compassion. Unity in the church is unity in Christ, and this unity transcends all human differences.

---

[3]Rowan Williams, Enthronement Sermon, Canterbury Cathedral: February 27, 2003, www.archbishop.ogr/sermonsspeeches/o30227.html downloaded February 28, 2003.
[4]Ibid.
[5]Ibid.
[6]Ibid.

BIBLIOGRAPHY

"Canterbury and Wales Celebrate Holy Cross Day at the Commencement of the ACC meeting in Hong Kong." ACNS 3129-ACC12 Media Release No2-14, September 2002. ACNS-admin@www.stormcentre.net. Accessed 21 September, 2002.

Bates, Stephen. "New Mission for Man of Many Talents" *Guardian Unlimited/Special reports*, July 24, 2002 (Downloaded September 12, 2002). Available from http:www.guardian.co.uk/religion/Story/0,2673,762065,00.html.

Evans, Jill. *Beloved and Chosen: Women of Faith.* Norwich: The Canterbury Press, 1993.

Gledhill, Ruth. "Archbishop fires opening shot at Disney" *Timesonline,* http://www.timesonline.co.uk.print, July 23, 2002. Downloaded Sept. 26, 2002.

Handley, Paul. "The Patron Saint of Disruption" *The Independent on Sunday* December 1, 2002.

Hattersley, Roy. "Just Williams" *Guardian*, July 11, 2004. Available from www.guardian.co.uk/print/0,3858,4968374-103602,00.html

Holloway, Richard, ed. *The Anglican Tradition*, Wilton, Connecticut: Morehouse-Barlow, 1984.

Holmes, Urban T. III, *What is Anglicanism.* Wilton, Connecticut: Morehouse-Barlow, 1982.

Kirby, Alex. "The Challenges facing the New Archbishop" *BBC News/UK,* July 23, 2002, downloaded October 4, 2002 from http://news.co.uk./1/hi/uk/213088.stm.

Koenig, Elisabeth. "Rowan Williams & the Seminary Classroom." *The Anglican* 31, no. 4 (October, 2002): 5-9.

Leech, Ken. "The Dispute about Rowan." *Jubilee Group* Miscellaneous paper. October 2002; available from http://www.anglocatholic.socialism.org.rowandispute.html; Internet; accessed 18 January, 2003.

Neil, Stephen. *Anglicanism.* New York: Oxford University Press, 1977.

McGrath, Alister. "Alister McGrath on Rowan Williams." The Anglican Digest, Advent 2002, 56-62.

Rowell, Geoffrey. The English Religious Tradition and the Genius of Anglicanism. Nashville: Abingdon press, 1992.

Rowell, Geoffrey. *The Vision Glorious.* Oxford: Oxford University Press, 1983.

Shortt, Rupert. *Rowan Williams: An Introduction.* London: Darton, Longman & Todd, 2003.

Southern, Humphrey "The Impossibility of the Last Word: The Theology of Rowan Williams," Anglicans Together (downloaded June 7, 2004). Available from http://www.anglicanstogether.org3.html.

Thomas, Cal. "The Great Welch Disappointment" *Townhall.com,* September 2, 2002 (downloaded May 31, 2004). Available from http://www.townhall.com/columnists/ calthomas /printct20020902.shtml.

Turner, Graham. "Four Twists in a Canterbury Tale," *newstelegraph.co.telegraph.co.us,* March 30, 2002. Downloaded November 4, 2002.

Webb, William J. *Slaves, Women and Homosexuals: Exploring the Hermeneutics of Cultural Analysis.* Downers Grove, Illinois: InterVarsity Press, 2001.

Williams, Gary J. "The Theology of Rowan Williams: An Outline Critique and Consideration of it's Consequences.*" Latimer Studies*; available from www.latimertrust.org; Internet; accessed 12, December, 2002.

Williams, Rowan. *A Ray of Darkness.* Cambridge, Massachusetts: Cowley Publications, 1995.

_____. *Arius: Heresy and Tradition.* Grand Rapids, Michigan: Wm. B. Eerdmans, 001.

_____. *Christian Spirituality: A Theological History from the New Testament to Luther and St. John of the Cross.* Atlanta: John Knox Press, 1980.

_____. *Lost Icons: Reflections on Cultural Bereavement.* New York: Morehouse Publishing, 2000.

_____. *On Christian Theology.* Oxford, England: Blackwell Publishers, 2001.

_____. *Ponder These Things: Praying with Icons of the Virgin.* Franklin, Wisconsin: Sheed & Ward, 2002.

_____. *Resurrection: Interpreting the Easter Gospel.* London: Darton, Longman and Todd Publishers, 1982.

_____. *Theresa of Avila.* London: Continuum, 1991.

_____. *The Wound of Knowledge: A Theological History from the New Testament to Luther and St. John of the Cross.* Eugene, Oregon: Wipf and Stock Publishers, 1998.

Williams, Rowan, ed. *The Making of Orthodoxy: Essays in Honour of Henry Chadwick.* Cambridge: Cambridge University Press, 1989.

_____, ed. *Sergii Bulgakov: Towards a Russian Political Theory.* Edinburgh: T & T Clark Ltd., 1999.

Williams, Rowan. "Authority and the Bishop in the Church." In *Their Lord and Ours: Approaches to Authority, Community and the Unity of the Church*, ed. Mark Santer, 90-110. London: SPCK, 1982.

_____. "Dark Night of the Soul." In *The New Dictionary of Pastoral Studies*, ed. Wesley Carr, 84. London: SPCK, 2002.

_____. "Mysticism." In *The New Dictionary of Pastoral Studies*, ed. Wesley Carr, 229. London: SPCK, 2002.

_____. "Resurrection." In *The New Dictionary of Pastoral Studies*, ed. Wesley Carr, 315-316. London: SPCK, 2002.

_____. "Trinity." In *The New Dictionary of Pastoral Studies*, ed. Wesley Carr, 381-382. London: SPCK, 2002.

_____. "Catholicity." In *The Oxford Companion to Christian Thought*, ed. Adrian Hastings, Alistair Mason and Hugh Pyper, 102-104. Oxford:Oxford University Press, 2000.

_____. "Resurrection." In *The Oxford Companion to Christian Thought*, ed. Adrian Hastings, Alistair Mason and Hugh Pyper, 616-618. Oxford:Oxford University Press, 2000.

_____. "Teaching the Truth." In *Living Tradition: Affirming Catholicism in the Anglican Church,* ed. Jeffrey Johns, 29-43. Boston: Cowley Publication, 1992.

_____. "Theology and the Churches." In *Michael Ramsey as Theologian*, ed. Robin Gill and Lorna Kendall. Boston: Cowley Publications. 1995.

_____.Enthronement Sermon, Canterbury Cathedral: February 27, 2003, www.archbishop.ogr/ sermonsspeeches/030227.html downloaded February 28, 2003.

_____. "The Seal of Orthodoxy": Mary and the Heart of Christian Doctrine," *Say Yes to God: Mary and the Revealing of the Word Made Flesh* ed. Martin Warner London: Tufton Books, 1999.

_____. *Mandate* Vol. 25, number 5 (September/October 2002): 16.

"A Statement by the Primates of the Anglican Communion meeting in Lambeth Palace" Oct.16, 2003.

www.ingramcontent.com/pod-product-compliance
Lightning Source LLC
Chambersburg PA
CBHW060347100426
42812CB00003B/1160